| DATE | | | |
|---|---|---|---|
| | | | |
| | | | |
| | | | |
| | | | |
| | | | |
| | | | |
| | | | |
| | | | |
| | | | |
| | | | |
| | | | |
| | | | |

# THE BRASS-TACKS ENTREPRENEUR

# THE
# BRASS-TACKS
# ENTREPRENEUR

JIM SCHELL

HENRY HOLT AND COMPANY / NEW YORK

*To Mary,*
*my friend, business partner, and wife,*
*who encouraged me to rediscover*
*a long-forgotten love affair*
*with the written word.*

Henry Holt and Company, Inc.
*Publishers since 1866*
115 West 18th Street
New York, New York 10011

Henry Holt® is a registered
trademark of Henry Holt and Company, Inc.

Published in Canada by Fitzhenry & Whiteside Ltd.,
91 Granton Drive, Richmond Hill, Ontario L4B 2N5.

Library of Congress Cataloging-in-Publication Data
Schell, Jim.
The brass-tacks entrepreneur / Jim Schell.—1st ed.
p.    cm.
Includes index.
1. New business enterprises—Management.   2. Small business—
Management.   3. Success in business.   I. Title.
HD62.5.S33      1993
658.4'21—dc20                                    92-32399
                                                    CIP

ISBN 0-8050-2370-4

First Edition—1993

Designed by Katy Riegel

Printed in the United States of America
All first editions are printed on acid-free paper. ⊗

10   9   8   7   6   5   4   3   2   1

# CONTENTS

*Acknowledgments*                                           xi
*Foreword*                                                  xiii

## I.  SMALL BUSINESS EVOLUTION                              1

1. Not Every Small Businessman Is an
   Entrepreneur                                             3
2. The Three Phases of Evolution                            7
3. Case History of Phase I, the UPS Years                  11
4. Case History of Phase II, the Sunshine Years            15
5. Case History of Phase III, the Years from Hell          19
6. Case History of the Sale                                24

## II.  THE START-UP                                        29

7. The Business Plan                                       31
8. Financing                                               36
9. Details                                                 42

## III.  THE INSIDE PLAYERS                                45

10.  Product Champion                                      47
11.  Financial Person                                      50
12.  Someone to Pick Up the Pieces                         54


## IV.  THE OUTSIDE PLAYERS                                57

13.  Mentors                                               59
14.  Bankers                                               62
15.  Lawyers                                               67
16.  Accountants                                           70
17.  The Board of Directors                                75
18.  Consultants                                           78
19.  Spouses                                               81


## V.  THE KEYS TO SUCCESS                                 83

20.  Team Building and Collecting Superstars               85
21.  Customer Reverence                                    88
22.  A Commitment to Quality                               94
23.  Employee Ownership                                    99
24.  The Right Niche                                      103
25.  A Balanced Culture                                   106
26.  Clarity                                              110
27.  Accountability                                       113
28.  Compensation                                         116
29.  Training                                             122
30.  Communications                                       126
31.  Coping with Change                                   132


## VI.  ORIGINS OF THE MOST PAINFUL MISTAKES             137

32.  Hiring                                               139
33.  Firing                                               144
34.  Cash Flow                                            148
35.  Inventory                                            151
36.  Expense Control                                      155

37. Focus                                       159
38. Strategy and Planning                        162
39. Conflict Avoidance                           167
40. Crisis Management                            170
41. The Peter Principle                          173

**VII.  CAREER DECISIONS**                       175

42. Entrepreneur or Manager?                     177
43. Private or Public?                           180

**VIII.  SELLING THE BUSINESS**                  185

44. The Process                                  187
45. Due Diligence                                195
46. The Purchase Agreement                       199
47. The Unwritten Rule of Cash                   202
48. After the Sale                               205

**IX.  THE ENTREPRENEUR: WHO WE ARE AND
WHY WE PERSEVERE**                               209

49. The Ingredients We Need to Survive           211
50. The Stereotypical Entrepreneur               218
51. The Ultimate Upside                          221
52. The Ultimate Downside                        224
53. Entrepreneurial Terror                       227
54. Why We Endure                                229

**X.  TIPS FOR SUCCESS**                         233

55. My Top Twelve Tips                           235

**XI.  EPILOGUE**                                239

56. In Defense of the Entrepreneur               241

*Index*                                          245

# ACKNOWLEDGMENTS

A special thanks to Tom Moe, Randy Duncan, Larry Fleming, Jake Nordstrom, and Stuart Amos for their introductions; Harvey McKay for his instructions; and Sue Johnson for her preparations.

# FOREWORD

THERE ARE 6 million working entrepreneurs in the United States. Another 750,000 wannabes will open their doors this year, while failure, retirement, and sell-out take their toll on a similar number.

The majority of us, survivors and wannabes, have entered, or will enter, our entrepreneurial careers unprepared for the perils of our profession. We are, or will be, accidental entrepreneurs, untrained and unsophisticated. We start up our business because, well, it seems like the thing to do at the time. Maybe we discover we can't work for anybody else, or maybe we think the world needs another widget, or maybe we stumble on an undiscovered niche. It just happens.

I learned the tricks of the entrepreneurial trade the way most of us do, at the costly and unforgiving hands of trial and error. Too independent to ask for help, too crusty to listen, and too busy to take the time, I plodded onward, discovering old and painful truths with each forward step. Over the course of my career I made the same needless, energy-draining mistakes that entrepreneurs have continued to make since the day that small business's tent was originally pitched.

I needed help. Someone to hold my hand. Someone who had been there before. Someone to help me avoid the endless list of unnecessary mistakes that are part of our profession, and someone to help me recover from those I couldn't escape.

I needed a mentor.

And you need one, too. I want to be your mentor. You provide the energy and the capital, and I'll add the answers and the solutions.

My qualifications? I've survived twenty-two years as a card-carrying entrepreneur, including four private and successful start-ups. The last of the four grew to a $25 million company, complete with two hundred employees and all the attendant trauma that comes with rapid growth. Over those years I've seen just about everything that can happen to a privately held small business, from incubation through acquisition.

*The Brass-Tacks Entrepreneur* will share the lessons of my successes and failures and provide you with the mentor I never had.

In the early chapters of the book, utilizing an abbreviated case-history approach, I discuss the evolutionary stages of the entrepreneurial business, as I prepare you for the "how-to" and "what-it's-like" lessons that will follow. And then it's on into the world of hands-on experience. We'll take a look at the business start-up, the inside and outside players that make up our entrepreneurial environment, the keys to our success, the origins of our most painful mistakes, the make-it-or-break-it decisions we face, and on through the sale of our company. Finally comes an introspective look at the species *entrepreneur,* in an attempt to give the wannabes among you some idea of what it takes to become one.

Why should I, who never had a mentor myself, want to become yours?

Because I'm offended by the unending waste that is a natural by-product of the trial-and-error method of learning. Because I'm offended by the cost of that waste to us, our shareholders, and our employees. Because I'm offended by the inevitable burnout that is bound to take its toll as a result of our mistakes. And because I want to help you avoid the mistakes I made, learn from the successes I enjoyed, and purge trial and error from your collection of management tools.

Oh yes, a note to the female reader. Most of the time, I have used the pronoun *his.* I could just as well have used *her . . .* strike a blow to tradition. Or I could just as well have used *his/her . . .* strike a blow to improved prose. I hope you'll understand.

Entrepreneuring will never be a stress-free vocation. Often lonely and always endangered, we hover eternally on the financial edge, with Chapter 11 and personal bankruptcy no further than a banker's phone call away.

But it sure beats the hell out of punching clocks. And saying yessir when we really mean nosir, and politicking and schmoozing and covering our footsteps when we would rather be creating and growing and taking new strides.

And I must warn you, entrepreneuring is addictive. I hated it occasionally, loved it usually, and needed it always. And I wouldn't trade professions with anybody, except for Arnold Palmer.

And finally, someone once said that every person, to be happy, needs something or somebody to love, a place to work, and a dream to pursue. This book is about all three.

# ENTREPRENEURSHIP IS:

*The ultimate responsibility, because our employees and families are so dependent upon our success.*

*The ultimate adventure, because the cost of failure is so severe.*

*The ultimate opportunity, because the upside has so few limitations.*

# I

## SMALL BUSINESS
## EVOLUTION

# 1

## NOT EVERY
## SMALL BUSINESSMAN IS
## AN ENTREPRENEUR

WHAT DO STEVEN Jobs, Seymour Cray, Ted Turner, and Mr. Matulef have in common?

The correct answer is that these four men are, or were, by common definition anyway, entrepreneurs. There are significant differences, however, between Mr. Matulef and the other three gentlemen.

I was weaned on Mr. Matulef's groceries. He was our friendly neighborhood grocer in 1940, peddling his wares four blocks from my boyhood home in Des Moines. I can still recall standing at the age of eight with my mother in Matulef's bread lines.

Matulef was not privy to today's business literature with its "revere the customer" doctrine. Somehow he had learned for himself that neighborhood housewives were his, uh, bread and butter. He treated my mother and her peers as if he owed them his livelihood. Matulef would walk the bread line in front of his store, exchanging news and tidbits with my mother and his other regular customers.

I left Des Moines after high school and have no idea what happened to Matulef. The last time I returned, a jewelry store stood where his grocery store once was. I do know I haven't seen a Matulef's chain competing with the Safeways, Alpha Betas, and Piggly Wigglys of the world.

Matulef, I would guess, never knew an investment banker. I'm sure he never considered an IPO or mezzanine debt with equity kickers. He may have had a bookkeeper (probably Mrs. Matulef), but never a controller or a CFO. His primary concerns were the freshness of his vegetables and the rent check due on Friday. His only motivations were to feed his family, keep his customers happy, and assure that his grocery suppliers continued to send their trucks his way. Directors' meetings, equity searches, and the squelching of hostile takeovers did not distract Matulef from running his business.

Compare Mr. Matulef to entrepreneurial sex symbol Steven Jobs as he prepares his business plan for Next. Jobs's financing includes a complex tangle of equity and debt. Shareholders, bankers, and even old competitors are in on the deal. Product rollouts are planned: M.B.A.'s and industry superstars are hired amid a flurry of corporate intrigue and financial sleight-of-hand. Media leaks are orchestrated, and the band plays on.

Matulef and Jobs do their entrepreneurial thing in two different worlds.

I've had an ongoing problem with the word *entrepreneur* ever since people started calling me one twenty years ago. I looked it up. *Webster's* informs us that an entrepreneur is "a person who organizes and manages a business undertaking, assuming the risk for the sake of profits." In *Webster's* eyes, Jobs and Matulef are both entrepreneurs.

Well, not in mine.

The word *entrepreneur* is far too sexy for the things that Matulef did. Matulef was a grinder, a mucker. He unloaded trucks, swept the office, signed checks, and directed his bookkeeper, all in the course of a day's sweaty business. Matulef lifted and toted and toiled.

Jobs meanwhile meets with R & D, teleconferences with investment bankers, and confers with venture capitalists, all between sessions with the advertising agency. Jobs delegates and dictates and commands.

Matulef's primary business contacts were mailmen, truck drivers, and bank tellers. Jobs's are investment bankers, venture capitalists, and presidents of just about everything.

Today's perception of the word *entrepreneur* fits Jobs: sexy, mystifying, exotic.

But it doesn't work for Matulef. His daily tasks require a more basic, blue-collar word. Should we consider the word *guess-man*, representing the manner in which his business decisions were usually reached? Or maybe *trial-and-errorist* for the business systems that he employed? How about *elbow-greaser* for the manner in which Matulef completed his daily chores?

My favorite? *Seat-of-the-pantser.* The Gospel of Basic Business Strategies According to Matulef: no policy manuals, no precedents, no logical order. As in, straight from the seat of the pants. OK, *seat-of-the-pantser* is too long, with too many syllables. We'll shorten it to *pantser.*

Still fuzzy on the difference between pantsers and entrepreneurs? Maybe this will help:

| PANTSER | ENTREPRENEUR |
|---|---|
| Meets with employees at corner tavern | Meets with board of directors in Hawaii |
| Has a bookkeeper | Has CFO (or controller, or tax adviser, or all of above) |
| Balances the checkbook | Manages cash |
| Reacts | Plans |
| Rolls the dice | Consults |
| Risks it all | Risks the business |
| Fulfills needs | Pursues dreams |

Pantsers can, and often do, evolve into entrepreneurs. This transition occurs when their primary business motivation ceases to be survival and sustenance and shifts instead to creativity and growth. Conversely, there are those not-so-pleasant times when established entrepreneurs must revert to pantsers, as their northbound plans head south.

I was a graduate pantser myself. Pantsering, I can attest, is not the quickest, easiest, or most efficient manner in which to build a business. I struggled and strained and rewrote the rules of business for ten years before finally graduating to entrepreneur. Looking back, I wish I had achieved entrepreneurship earlier—there were too many wasted years in between.

In later years when my company was growing at a 30 percent annualized pace, I would enviously eye the managerial tools the corporate bailouts or college-trained entrepreneurs could bring to the small business table. God knows I could have used their management skills and financial expertise.

But pantsering was my life. It was sometimes painful, often lonely, and always inefficient. But it paid the bills, beat the hell out of working for somebody else, and gave me a unique, from-the-bottom-up view of the business world.

A view that the M.B.A.'s and corporate guys will never have.

### THE BOTTOM LINE

The pantser is an unsophisticated, entry-level small business owner and is not to be confused with the more sophisticated entrepreneur. The pantser's primary business motivations are survival and sustenance, the entrepreneur's creativity and growth.

The pantser peers at the business world from the basement. In later years this subterranean view will provide a grass-roots understanding of the role of customers and employees in the business equation.

# 2

---

# THE THREE PHASES
# OF EVOLUTION

---

SUCCESSFUL SMALL BUSINESSES do not just happen. They evolve. Those of us caught up in the day-to-day chaos of small business growth do not recognize the logical process of evolution until it has passed. Rather, we view the ongoing mess as some kind of disjointed sequence of random events, crisis after never-ending crisis.

And so it was in my pantser days. I was always too busy to step back and plot my company's evolution and too unsophisticated to know what I should be listening for. Each day, and each year, was another series of knee-jerk reactions, reactions to the events of yesterday with no understanding of what was coming tomorrow.

There are, however, identifiable patterns to business growth. George T. Ainsworth-Land, in his book *Grow or Die* (Wiley, 1986), discusses the subject of business evolution in detail. Land, one of those strategic planners about whom we read in the business periodicals, tells us the evolution of a business includes three phases:

**Phase I: Entrepreneurial**
**Phase II: Norming**
**Phase III: Integrating**

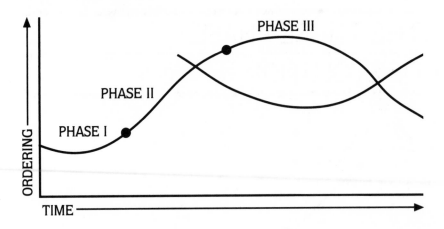

Every company, Ainsworth-Land tells us, spends varying amounts of time in Phases I and II, moving eventually into Phase III if it survives the two earlier stages. Phase I is the start-up stage, that early period when the entrepreneur/pantser dominates the scene. From there the company moves into Phase II, or the Norming stage, as the business achieves a degree of order (and profitability). Finally, growth propels the maturing company into the turmoil of Phase III, where it either makes the necessary changes to begin a new phase of its life cycle (back to a new Phase I, thus restarting the cycle) or, if the necessary concessions to growth aren't made, becomes another name in the small business obits.

The amount of time spent in each of these three phases will vary from business to business. Factors such as the rate of sales growth, the quality and depth of management, the strength of the niche, and the aggressiveness of the competition will determine the length of time spent in each phase and the degree of difficulty experienced therein.

So what? you ask.

Well, for starters it is reassuring to those of us caught up in the growth of our business to know there is a preordained order to the chaos we are experiencing. More important, advance knowledge of the formidable (and inevitable) Phase III can assist us in planning for, and minimizing the impact of, this entrepreneurial equivalent of the Great Depression.

Read a few pages of Ainsworth-Land's book and you can quickly identify him as theorist, scientist, and intellectual. I doubt that he would have put up with pantsering for more than a week. I can't envision him closing up the store after hours, vacuuming the office on Sunday, chasing a shoplifter, dunning a slow payer, or looking over his shoulder while making the midnight deposit. Most of all, I can't see him allowing his company to suffer through a prolonged and painful Phase III.

In spite of my perception of Ainsworth-Land's no-sweat background, I agree with his description of the three phases, but not his terminology. You had to have been there, and I suspect Ainsworth-Land wasn't. So while acknowledging his theory, I have rechristened his three phases with names suitable for, and understandable to, us galley slaves who are veterans of the voyage. Had Ainsworth-Land been alongside us manning the oars, he would understand.

Phase I: The UPS Years
Phase II: The Sunshine Years
Phase III: The Years from Hell

The following chapters briefly trace the nineteen-year life span of my fourth and last company, National Screenprint, as I tie its evolution and growth to Ainsworth-Land's three phases of growth. These chapters are designed to give warning, relief, and hope to those readers who are sloshing and sweating through one of these phases as we speak.

## THE BOTTOM LINE

There is a predictable but not-so-orderly evolution in the growth of the entrepreneurial small business. The entrepreneur/pantser, recognizing his company's location in that evolution, can plan for and minimize the downside effects or maximize the upside opportunities of the approaching phase.

Most important is the anticipation of and preparation for the potential catastrophe of Phase III: the Years from Hell.

# 3

## CASE HISTORY OF PHASE I, THE UPS YEARS

*National Screenprint was started in 1972 on a $15,000 invest-
ment. Two college students, working between classes, were its
first employees. The company screenprinted athletic uniforms,
jerseys, and T-shirts in a south Minneapolis basement. The
niche was solid and promised future opportunities. The customer was the sporting-goods dealer, the service was screenprinting, and the tech was low. The company's employees were young
and inexperienced and the balance sheet weak and anemic. Par
for the entrepreneurial course.*

THE UPS (United Parcel Service) drivers that I have known always
treated their customers like, well, customers, the way Mr. Matulef
treated my mother. As if they were important, as if they mattered.
This attitude even existed in the early seventies, before Peters and
his contemporaries made the "revere the customer" theory fash-
ionable. Today, this degree of responsiveness to customers is
downright necessary for UPS, given the extreme competition
within its industry, but twenty years ago it was a welcome bonus
to those of us on the receiving end. (It made things easier, I suppose, that the U.S. Postal Service set the industry standards.)

UPS employees seem to have a personal stake in the performance of their job, just as we pantsers must have in ours. I often
fantasized, as I watched our UPS driver efficiently go about his

duties, that someday my employees would display a similar work ethic and sense of urgency in accomplishing theirs.

The UPS driver's attitude and the manner in which he goes about his duties cement the bond and intensify the respect that exists between him and the pantser. His dedication, his dependability, and his lack of wasted motion are the traits we look for in our own employees. The UPS driver is a symbol of these early Phase I days when driver and pantser often work together side by side on the loading dock, trading jokes and packages.

After all, UPS and mail delivery rank as two highlights of the pantser's day. When the unsightly brown truck bleats its greeting, the ongoing chores are temporarily interrupted. All important hands scurry on deck to rummage frantically through the day's packaged goodies, looking for resolutions to the latest crisis.

The UPS driver is only one of the outsiders who are strategically important to the hands-on pantser. Others include the landlord, the banker, and the accounts payable clerks of those vendors who oversee our substitution of vendor credit for bank borrowing. We deal with them all, face to face, eyeball to eyeball, as our company crawls and stumbles through its early years of growth.

And, of course, there are our customers. We Phase I pantsers know them all—by first name. They keep us informed of our industry's trends better than any employee ever could. Ten years from now, unhappily, sales managers and account executives and the many levels of management will separate us from our customers. Occasional sales calls will have to suffice, with salespeople stiffly leading the way as we strive to stay in front of our customers as well as on top of our business. But it will never be the same.

These UPS Years are the uncomplicated, hands-on part of the entrepreneurial life cycle, an integral part of the learning process. The M.B.A.'s and the corporate highfliers will never know the guts of their business the way we Phase I pantsers know ours. There is no one in the middle to muddy the view. We are a part of the assembly process, we see the service or product delivered, the invoice rendered. We hold out our hand and payment is received. Thanks for your business, we acknowledge with a smile, and have a nice day.

The work is hard, the sweaty and physically draining kind of hard. The hours are long and sometimes tedious, but by the end of the day we can see, touch, and feel the progress we have made. The gratification is instantaneous.

When there is a glitch, we fix it. There is no delegation, no excuses, no finger-pointing along the way. Communications are nose to nose, no politics exist to impede our progress. Rewards and setbacks are immediate.

Surprises are infrequent and never as traumatic as in later years when we become the pawns of processed information and the various levels of management. In the UPS phase we are close enough to each of the key components of our business to anticipate any startling news tomorrow's financial statements might yield. In later years, when those financial statements can, and will, spew out the cruelest of tidings with nary a warning, we will yearn for the UPS Years, when results were predictable. And timely.

I loved the directness and immediate gratification that came as a result of my day's labors. My midwestern work ethic was at its best in those years, and I could see and feel that my effort made the difference. Delegation, motivation, reward, and punishment were simple, direct, and quick.

I hated the mistakes that we made in those days—mistakes that came from inexperience and mistakes that wasted finite resources. I hated the process of trial and error and the toll it took. I hated the incessant details and the lack of human and financial resources to handle them, especially in those areas not related to the conduct of business (insurance, government regulations, and an endless list of administrative and personnel issues). I hated the time it took to resolve what I perceived to be minor-league problems, like trying to understand workmen's comp and how vacation pay accrues, at the expense of major-league opportunities like developing products and servicing customers. If I wasn't making things happen, nobody was, and I hated my lack of leverage.

Corporate culture has its roots in those early UPS Years. Many of our pantser attitudes, pearls of practical wisdom at the time, remain with our company forever, or at least until we decide to change them. We develop cultural attitudes toward the role of the sales force, the perception of the customer, the degree of dedication to service and quality, the importance of ethics in our business relationships, and the depth of our concern for employees. Each of these attitudes, crucial components in the success or failure of small businesses and Fortune 500 companies alike, begins at the loading dock with our friend the UPS driver looking on.

Twenty years later survivors of the UPS Years (and there won't be many) will remember those days as the best of all. Employees who weren't among the pioneers will be forced to listen to countless eye-rolling hours of exaggerated tales of corporate history.

Like boot camp and spring training, the UPS Years are tedious and trying. They are, however, necessary to the success of the entrepreneur and the team. The arrival of the Sunshine Years (Phase II) will officially signify the end of the Phase I journey (none too soon for most of us), and usher in another assortment of challenges for the recently crowned entrepreneur. The challenges of Phase II will have to be met with a new set of managerial responses that will not come naturally to those of us accustomed to doing things our way.

By the time the UPS Years have passed, someone else will be standing on the loading dock, greeting that ugly, brown truck. The pantser makes way for the entrepreneur.

## THE BOTTOM LINE

The UPS Years are the formative years for the company and its founder. They are Business 101, the basics of the small business game. No business can graduate to the Sunshine Years without passing through this sweat-stained time.

Much of the corporate culture that will become a part of the company has its roots in the UPS Years. The pantser should make sure that the cultural messages he sends to his employees during these times are consistent with his vision of the adult corporation. Corporate culture, once established, is not easily changed.

# 4

# CASE HISTORY OF PHASE II, THE SUNSHINE YEARS

*National Screenprint's sales and profits grew steadily, and the company subsequently opened production centers in Madison, Wisconsin, and Denver, in addition to the Minneapolis location.*

*The first CFO was hired as sales reached $5 million. Five new production centers were added in the next seven years. By 1983 sales had reached $9 million as the company gained a reputation for creativity and service in a new niche—providing imprinted sportswear to department stores and mass merchandisers. Sales were about to explode in this new niche, along with receivables and inventory.*

*By the time National Screenprint's sales had reached $15 million, they were increasing at a 30 percent annualized rate. Cash flow was a continual problem, the balance sheet sagged, and management struggled to keep up.*

THE SUNSHINE YEARS began around the time our sales topped $5 million. I celebrated by hiring our first CFO. In truth, my pantser style had long since outlived its usefulness, but I found it difficult, often impossible, to let it go. Not until the workweeks could stretch no longer would I allow the pantser in me to fade and the entrepreneur and fledgling manager to emerge.

I was Walter Mitty on a roll during those early Sunshine Years and learned to love every cluttered minute. Today's opportunities turned into tomorrow's customers and frustrating bottlenecks into well-oiled systems. I learned to leverage my time and delegated many of my mundane pantser tasks to others. Nevertheless, the company was still small enough during the sunshine years for me to keep my hand firmly on its pulse. I alone controlled the growth and direction of our company.

The pantser's goal of survival and sustenance had been replaced by a dream. Visions of empires danced in my head.

The mistakes, confusion, and individual effort of the UPS Years bow to the optimism, growth, and profitability of the Sunshine Years. Key employees surface and productive teams appear. Satisfied old customers beget curious new ones. Orders for products or services appear as if from nowhere for destinations previously reserved for only the toughest and largest competitors.

Employees who were entry-level hires during the UPS Years take on important new roles during the Sunshine Years. Some keep pace with sales growth; a few excel. A consistent flow of good news results in new friendships and office camaraderie and beers after work. Peter and his unpleasant principle lurk nearby, no further away than our friends or relatives in adjoining offices, but even as the weakness of some employees surfaces, others step in to save the day and help postpone the tough decisions.

Increasing sales translate into increasing profits, the businessman's dream. The underfed balance sheet puts meat on its scraggly bones, and the welcome profits convert into fresh equity and spit out increased working capital. Borrowing bases grow, the balance sheet becomes banker-friendly, and the entrepreneurial company suddenly becomes a desirable customer for those with money to lend.

Successes during these early Sunshine Years exceed failures by a wide margin. We anticipate the arrival of the monthly financials and hopefully share them with anybody and everybody who has played key roles in the accomplishment. The continuous flow of good news serves as a reward for our efforts and a stimulant to our motivation. The business of doing business is fun, even as work hours stretch to the point where efficiency drops. The smell of victory is everywhere, and its sweet aroma keeps us on the playing field long after the game is over.

The bright optimism of the early Sunshine Years can blind all but the wariest of entrepreneurs and the most professional of managers. As the profits roll in we tend to overlook the need to continually upgrade both personnel and systems to allow us to process tomorrow's workload. Organization charts need refining, new positions need creating, commission schedules and production scheduling systems become outdated. Changes are overdue in such cultural attitudes as accountability, dedication to quality, and performance geared toward designated goals. Key employees need training, and sometimes culling.

But the numbers are still black and the future still rosy, and so we postpone the difficult decisions. Or look the other way.

As revenues continue their climb through the latter part of the Sunshine Years, new danger signals appear. Crises become bigger and take longer to resolve. Our trial-and-error–trained management teams are stretched dangerously thin, and support functions strain to keep up with sales. Employees bail out if they dislike the constant stress and pressure that comes with rapid growth, often leaving gaping holes in our team. Systems and controls that hummed at $5 million in sales sputter and cough at $10 million.

The waning stages of the Sunshine Years can also be darkened by the appearance of the cursed *I* word: *Inventory.* Old dataprocessing systems are no longer able to track the complicated inventory process as it winds from the purchase of raw materials, through order allocation, work-in-process, and finally the sale. Inventory accumulates, and cash becomes even more scarce.

As the Packers and the Steelers learned so many years ago, success has its cycles. The Sunshine cycle may be long or it may be short, but it is finite and we can depend on the fact that it will eventually pass. The quality of the players, the strength of the niche, the rate of sales growth, and the muscle of the balance sheet will ultimately determine the amount of sunshine to be enjoyed, but count on it: the clouds will appear.

Those of us with visions of empires must learn to see beyond the glow of the Sunshine Years. We must learn to study tomorrow's cash-flow projections more closely than yesterday's profit and loss statements. We must look for the bad news that threatens our future, as well as for the good news that congratulates our past. We must plan and prepare and project, and learn to delegate our day-to-day operational functions to others. We must hire right and fire right, and we must see that those employees who choose to stay with us are trained and prepared.

The time will eventually come when we can relax and reflect and remember the prosperity of the Sunshine Years. But that time should be dictated by us and not by a series of unfriendly events.

Phase III, the Years from Hell, is a series of unfriendly events.

## THE BOTTOM LINE

The Sunshine Years are characterized by a period of expanding sales and increasing profits.

Only the ablest of entrepreneurs have the foresight to look past the euphoria of Phase II and ready the company for the approaching Phase III.

The entrepreneur's primary function during Phase II should shift to developing strategy, and many of his day-to-day operational functions should be delegated to others. His number one responsibility should be preparing the company for the impending Years from Hell.

# 5

## CASE HISTORY OF PHASE III, THE YEARS FROM HELL

*National Screenprint's sales had reached $25 million by the end of 1989. Many of the nation's leading retailers were its customers. Sales gains were limited only by financial and managerial resources.*

*As sales spiraled so did bottlenecks. Cash disappeared, management weakened, quality suffered, systems broke down. New staff was hired (some contributed, some did not) and new systems were introduced (some functioned, some did not). The founder struggled to make the transition from entrepreneur to manager.*

*In the summer of 1989 the entrepreneur gave up his attempt to become the professional manager his company needed. He hired a president. Too late.*

I REMEMBER THE first time I learned of the existence of Phase III. The revelation came to me from a banker, during those days when bankers actually made the rounds prospecting for new business. Our sales were $15 million at the time and I had a similar number of problems. They were no longer the disguised opportunities of the Sunshine Years, they were honest-to-God *problems*.

This particular banker was a veteran of the small business wars and had observed many an entrepreneurial career during the course of his travels. As we lunched together that day, I enumerated my imposing list of headaches and frustrations.

"Jim," the banker nodded gravely when I had finished, "I am sorry to inform you that you are *there*."

"Where is 'there'?" I asked, in my supreme innocence.

"'There' is that stage of small business development where nothing seems to work anymore. Where you've outgrown many of the people and the systems that got you where you are today. It happens to everyone, I'm afraid, and my experience has been that it usually occurs at somewhere between $12 million and $25 million in sales. And that," he concluded, "is where 'there' is for you."

He picked up the lunch tab and extended his hand. I never saw the man again.

But he was right.

If only we had seen it coming.

Ainsworth-Land calls Phase III one of integration and diversification. The word *restructuring* might also fit. However, to the suffering insiders, the troops in the trenches, Phase III can be best described as the Years from Hell. Perhaps Year from Hell if management is up to the task, or even Months from Hell if capable management and planning are combined with controlled sales growth and a solid balance sheet.

By 1986 National Screenprint was sorely lacking in management depth as we concluded another year of reckless growth. And if that wasn't enough, we were about to embark on three more years of similar growth. Signs of our impending calamity were everywhere, and by the time our sales had topped $18.5 million, we were firmly mired in the quicksand of our own personalized version of "there": the Years from Hell.

These are the years when the systems and controls that have sufficed for years are no longer adequate. When increased sales mean increased red ink. When financial statements yield surprise after eye-opening surprise, none of them pleasant. Murphy's Law rules the land.

The severity of the impact of the Years from Hell will depend largely on the rate of sales growth and the ability of management to adapt to the required strategic changes that need to be made.

The more rapid the sales growth, the more difficult it becomes to adapt. A 5 percent sales growth rate provides ample time to learn and react. A 35 percent sales growth rate and the accompanying crush of associated new problems do not.

A significant number of managers and key employees will not adjust to rapid sales growth; the pace and the problems will overwhelm them. Some of these failing employees joined the company in its incubation days. Some may be friends of the founder and some, God forbid, relatives.

Lack of employee growth in the face of rapid change, and the inevitable turnover that will result, manifests itself in many ways. Most devastating is the failure of corporate systems and controls—those systems and controls that, without the necessary upgrading, will shudder to a halt as the demand upon them exceeds their capability. These breakdowns are indiscriminate, and occur in computer networks, paper-flow systems, quality control, inventory control, credit policies, and collection of receivables. Even the most basic accounting systems are bound to spring leaks. Nothing is safe, little is spared.

Employee morale is the next to go, as the performance of those employees who cannot keep up affects the performance of those who can. And those employees who do continue to carry their weight become frustrated in an environment where their own efficiency, their department's performance, and the success of the team are restrained by the inadequacies of others.

OK, so Phase III is inevitable. But it doesn't have to last for three years, as it did for me, and it doesn't have to be hell, as it was for me. Instead, it could be a few months of minor inconvenience—maybe 4.0 on the Richter scale instead of the Big One. A blip on the screen instead of a spike.

Following are five damage-control measures that should be implemented to minimize the effects of the Years from Hell:

**1.** Here is the number one rule of surviving the Years from Hell. Do not—read my lips—do not throw more sales at the problem. Increased sales will only magnify existing deficiencies. Forget focusing on sales growth, focus instead on upgrading employees and repairing and restructuring the company's support systems.

**2.** A "strategic" change is needed, in the company and in the entrepreneur. Increased dosages of the same thing that brought on the problems in the first place will only make things worse. The normal method of entrepreneurial problem-solving—longer hours, gritted teeth, and increased adrenaline—is no longer enough.

Missions, goals, cultures, and strategies must be evaluated and upgraded. Systems and controls must be repaired or, more often, replaced. The organizational structure must be modernized. Most important, key employees must be inventoried and often, alas, replaced. Including, when the shoe fits, the entrepreneur himself.

**3.** Do not give managers and key employees aspirin (books and one-day seminars) when they require penicillin (consultants, schooling, and ongoing training). A fight for life is going on here, and the fight will be won or lost by the employees. The more help they get, the better the odds.

**4.** Be willing to go outside the organization for management help. A promote-from-within strategy in the face of exploding sales means content employees, and a cozy, secure, unthreatened corporate culture. It also means that the days of the company's existence are numbered.

**5.** Hire for tomorrow, not for today. The question is not, "Can the prospective employee do the job that exists today?" Rather it is, "Can he or she perform the tasks of tomorrow?"

As a pantser, and later as an entrepreneur, we are creating a living, breathing organism that provides products, opportunities, and careers. Our tools have been, to this point, sweat, dedication, guts, and the stimulation that comes from the pursuit of our dream.

But a new set of tools is needed now. Guts and sweat and dreams are no longer enough.

It is the entrepreneur that must make the most radical changes as we attempt to lead our company through and beyond those Years from Hell. Words like *focus* and *accountability* and *clar-*

*ity* and *balance* must be added to our vocabulary and to the inventory of our skills. Often soft and manipulative, these skills usually run counter to our normal way of doing things. They are, however, necessary if we are to develop into the leader and manager necessary to pull the company out of the depths of the Years from Hell. These soft skills are required to mold teams, motivate employees, and get things done in a new environment where the entrepreneur's role as a doer has changed to that of a delegator.

The managerial skills we need to lead our company are not developed overnight. We must make the choice, sometime during the course of the Sunshine Years, either to become the professional manager our growing company needs or to hire one.

The stake, as I would learn, is the company itself.

### THE BOTTOM LINE

Every company will pass through the Years from Hell. Anticipation of this period's approach, accompanied by advance planning, will determine the ultimate fate of the company and the entrepreneur.

Survival will be assured if the entrepreneur is willing to upgrade himself, the employees, and the systems and organizational structures, and then persevere until those changes are in place.

Failure to anticipate and plan for the Years from Hell can result in the sale of the company. Or worse.

# 6

## CASE HISTORY OF
## THE SALE

*National Screenprint was offered for sale in October of 1989. A letter of intent was signed the following February. On June 4, 1990, the company was sold.*
*The entrepreneur was not a part of the new owner's plans.*

THERE ARE TWO reasons why we make the decision to sell. Number one is because the mood strikes us. Number two is because we have a gun to our head, even if the gun is held in our own hand. I recommend selling because of the former.

I did it because of the latter.

Give even Bozo the Clown three nonstop years of unadulterated bad news and you won't see a smile on his face anymore. Entrepreneurial burnout can and will happen to those who allow the Years from Hell to drag on too long. Everybody's cup runneth over sooner or later.

The bad news of Phase III comes from everywhere once it begins to flow. P&Ls and balance sheets and cash-flow statements are automatic gut-wrenchers. Call the banker for a double dose of bad news. The CFO standing in the doorway has his lips poised for it. New sales are bad news, and so are no sales. Even random events do their bad-news best, as interest rates shoot up and competitors attack previously hallowed ground.

Once the bad news is on a roll, it fuels a change in everything we do. Burnout replaces enthusiasm, and early mornings are now for catching another five minutes of sleep or drinking a third cup of coffee. Offices are cold and lonely, devoid of good cheer. The hour hand on the office clock turns in perpetual slow motion. The hallowed after-hours beer becomes a piece of corporate history, and Saturdays are for TV and golf—just about anything except going to the office.

As the balance sheet is depleted, our ego dives along with it. Problems mount and solutions disappear. Work and pain become synonymous. Sleep and golf and vacations replace energy and enthusiasm and excitement. Escape lures us, and The Dream becomes The Nightmare.

Finally, total burnout arrives. We can't go on like this anymore. We inventory our options.

Scale back? It's too late, too hard, and anyway it won't solve our burnout problem, which reaches new depths every day.

Hire a president? Also too late, even if we could find, and afford, a good one.

Go public? Yeah, sure.

Equity injection? Me? Work for somebody else?

Thus we reach the only workable decision remaining: We sell.

We up and sell—lock, stock, barrel, and potted office plants. Everything we've worked for over the past twenty years. Here are the keys, here's the checkbook, here's the customer list. Have a nice life with my company.

And damned if it doesn't turn out to be the easiest thing we've ever done.

I'm not talking about the selling process being easy, because it isn't. Legions of lawyers will see to that (more on that subject in later chapters). What I'm talking about here is resolving the sale in our mind's eye.

The years of bad news have taken their toll. We may have been in the office, but our heart has moved on. There can be no regrets or seller's remorse after the spark is gone.

Don't believe it? Try unloading a towering mountain of debt sometime—overnight. Try putting some cash in a pocket where only IOUs and guarantees have rested before. Try turning three years of irate vendors' phone calls over to someone else. Stop studying the red entries in financial statements and shaking fingers at employees who try but can't deliver. Try putting an end forever to following up and being focused and making rational decisions and trying to make a multitude of changes that are unnatural to your basic self.

And most of all, try getting the hell out of an office that was a home for twenty years but a prison for the last three. Try doing something new and different, something you've always wanted to do but never had the time. Try freeing the creativity that has been imprisoned within you, ever since you began trying to become a structured and buttoned-down manager.

Try all of this, and see how it feels.

Then suck in a breath of freedom—freedom from organized organizations and structured structures. Freedom from rules and regulations that chafe and restrict. Freedom brought about by finally having a pocket full of cash instead of a file cabinet full of IOUs.

I never would have guessed I could leave my company without being pulled away, screaming and kicking. Nobody ever worked harder, nobody ever cared more. But, by God, I walked away, with eyes that were practically dry. That's what those Years from Hell can do.

Which is not to say that we won't have an emotional hangover as a result of the sale and our subsequent departure. Let's face it, we failed. We wanted to make the transition to professional manager but couldn't. Our adult corporation grew too big, too quickly. Our ego took a beating in the process, a beating that only time, and another success, can heal.

I fulfilled my role in the growth of my company. I gave it the leadership and direction it needed to emerge. I tugged and I pulled, and I watched the tyke take its first steps. Then I looked on in amazement as the youth grew into a teenager. And finally I watched that teenager become an adult, too complex and demanding for its entrepreneurial parent. The time finally came to hand over the reins to somebody else—a surrogate, a professional manager with a pocket full of focus, patience, and experience.

And cash.

Cash. Never the culprit, but always the messenger. For me, there was never enough of it, from the day twenty years ago when we scraped together $15,000 to open the doors, to my last day on the job when another $100,000 invoice came due. Most of us live with a shortage of cash for most of our entrepreneurial careers. We love it when we have enough (seldom) and hate it when we don't (often).

And so, it all comes down to this. Nature must take its inevitable course. Sooner or later everybody reaches their limitations. We have reached ours.

It's time to move on.

## THE BOTTOM LINE

The sale of the company does not have to have suicidal overtones; it can work to the advantage of everybody—the employees, the buyer, the entrepreneur. Everybody wins, if new management delivers the talent along with the cash.

Which is not to say the entrepreneur will walk away emotionally unscathed. No amount of compensation will make up for the fact that he was forced to sell as a result of his own shortcomings.

# II

## THE START-UP

# 7

## THE BUSINESS
## PLAN

A YOUNG FRIEND of mine had this crazy idea about opening an English pub in downtown Minneapolis. Short of cash, as most of my young friends always seem to be, he forwarded me his business plan. A first-time entrepreneur, he included in his bulky package a homemade prospectus, his plan in dizzying detail, and more financial projections than even the SBA could digest.

He was facing a tough sell, and he knew it. Bars and restaurants go up and come down faster than a Minneapolis thermometer in February. Investors are tough to find in this fragile and overcrowded niche.

But I coughed up some cash, more than I could afford at the time. Uncharacteristically, I might add; no one was more surprised than me. His plan was prepared so thoroughly and professionally I couldn't say no. If this was an indication of the way he would run his business, I concluded, I wanted a piece of the action.

The guy was no dummy. He knew that the primary purpose of a business plan is as a sales tool, and he needed investors, in a climate where investors were hard to find. The year was 1990, and the recession's foot was firmly set on American soil.

Folks with money to invest (or lend) are constantly exposed

to a wide variety of business plans as they search for deals. Their motive in reading a plan is as much to learn about the preparer as it is to understand the company. They recognize that the plan is the first official act of the new venture and rightfully assume the entrepreneur will manage their investment with the same diligence he used to prepare the plan.

People with money to lend attach more importance to the quality of the plan than to the content. They look for thoroughness and professionalism and attention to detail, in addition to the presentation of credible facts.

The sophisticated investor knows from experience it isn't the horse that wins the race but the jockey. That's the entrepreneur, the same guy who prepared the plan. If he put together a professional one, is it not logical that the investor can assume he will conduct his business in a similar fashion? (The converse assumption is equally true.)

A start-up business plan should include:

1. **The roster of players.** This is the first place the venture capitalists—professionals at reading (and rejecting) business plans—go. They want to know who is involved, what are their backgrounds, what are their goals? They want complete bios, including the entrepreneur's. Leave no key players unturned.
2. **The niche.** Include industry information, demographics, competitors, history, and projections for the future.
3. **The edge.** What does the product (or service) have that competitors do not?
4. **The risk.** Be up front and blunt. The investor's perception of the entrepreneur's honesty is key here. Downplaying the risks inherent in opening a business fools no one except those who are ripe to be fooled, like relatives and friends.
5. **The reward.** Include the expectations regarding dividends, reinvestment of profits, expansion, public offerings, and so on.
6. **Strategic issues.** Include your objectives for mission, goals, focus, customers, products, and employees.

7. **Financial projections.** Include P&Ls, balance sheets, and cash-flow statements. Project as far into the future as you wish, but forget making an issue of the exciting prospects for the year 2010. Those far-out, rose-colored guesstimates make good spreadsheet exercises, but most investors rarely look past year one. Long-range assumptions are too fuzzy to be meaningful.

8. **Sources of capital and credit.** If private, who are the current shareholders and/or who are the prospective investors? Interested investors want to know who their partners might be. In-place bank and vendor credit arrangements should be included as well.

9. **Compensation.** How will key employees be compensated? Include perks.

10. **Sales strategies.** Include pricing, distribution, and marketing strategies, as well as advertising and promotional plans.

11. **Miscellaneous.** Location, lease terms, future employee recruitment, names of legal and accounting firms, fixed assets required, prospective vendors, required licenses or agreements, committed and potential customers, competition, barriers to entry, product development, and so forth.

The complementary purpose of a business plan is to provide us with definition and focus through the start-up phase of our business. The plan should provide an initial path for us to follow, along with spelled-out goals to pursue.

The start-up entrepreneur should recognize that business plans are only operationally relevant on the day they are written, and with each passing day they become increasingly obsolete. An endless list of events, random and otherwise, conspire to antiquate them, often before the ink is dry.

Though they may be obsolete, they are never useless. The benefit of business plans, aside from their use in procuring investment, lies largely in the preparation and not in the product itself. A business plan serves as a tool to stimulate our thinking and forces us to consider options and strategies that we might not think of otherwise. Also, the very act of publishing the plan expresses our commitment, imprecise as it may be, to the process. After the plan is published, though it quickly loses its operational benefits, it still can be a barometer, a scorecard, and a measuring stick by which to rate our performance.

I have read that five- and ten-year plans are in corporate vogue, with some Japanese companies looking out as far as a hundred years. That may work for our big-business brethren, but it won't do the job for us. One year is about as far as I was able to go and realize any benefit from the results. (Entrepreneurial start-ups should not be confused with Fortune 500 companies' planning and strategy, and we should not be in any rush to adopt their mannerisms.)

We should adhere to the focus of our plans but never to the operations. We should be ready to make instant changes, to pursue whatever it was that happened yesterday, to follow whatever it might be that evolves tomorrow. Therein lies one of the entrepreneur's strengths.

There are as many different kinds of business plans as there are entrepreneurs. No two look alike. Local libraries carry a wealth of in-depth books on the process of writing a business plan. Small Business Development Centers offer seminars on business plans. (Most are located on college campuses. Call the SBDC Connection at 800-633-6450 for the SBDC nearest you.) Your accountants and attorneys retain drawersful of long-discarded plans prepared by your predecessors. Ask to see them, then use the best of the lot as a guide.

My English pub friend paid his first dividend exactly one year after pouring his first yard of ale. His second-year plan calls for— and current operations support—a 24 percent annual yield on my original investment.

Many events transpired during the course of that first year to cause a series of operational departures from his original plan and render it obsolete.

Nobody cared.

## THE BOTTOM LINE

The business plan is the first and the most important document the entrepreneur will ever prepare.

The degree of the start-up's potential will be perceived according to the quality of the plan.

The business plan also serves as a stimulant to the strategic planning process and as a written commitment to the entrepreneur's decisions.

Be responsive to the need to alter the plan. Herein lies one of the entrepreneur's most meaningful advantages over our corporate brethren.

# 8

---
# FINANCING
---

I'D LIKE TO ask you a question. If you think you know the answer, please raise your hand.

What is the number one cause of entrepreneurial failure?

(All hands shoot up at once.)

All right, so everybody knows that start-up cash—the lack of sufficient financing—is the number one cause of entrepreneurial failure.

So, if everybody knows it, then why does everybody continue to run out of it—year after painful year?

The answer is that we entrepreneurial types are an excitable sort. And a confident sort. And an optimistic sort. And we know damn well that our sweat and energy will conquer all, and so we enter the battle toting our rifles but leaving the ammunition behind.

Our niche is a cinch, we assure ourselves, and our timing is right. Anyway, we've never failed before; there's no reason why we should start now. A surge of energy accompanies our optimistic thoughts. Nothing can stop us. We find temporary financing thanks to a second mortgage perhaps, or maybe we sell the water-ski boat. Then we open our doors without permanent financing in place and wait for some banker/investor/angel/relative to see what he or she is missing. We'll worry later.

And then it's on into the guts of our venture. We hire somebody to sell it. And market it. And make it, and ship it, and bill it. We're movin' and shakin' now. Don't worry, we tell our employees, the financing will come.

But it doesn't. Oh, the sales do, but now we can't finance our new receivables. And we can't buy more inventory to replace what just turned into receivables that we can't carry any more of.

So what happens next? Our good employees get tired of working for nothing and with nothing. They hit the road.

We can't fill our new orders, so our hard-earned new customers follow our good employees out the door. And we can't pay our vendors, so we can't get enough product to ship to the customers who haven't walked out.

Then maybe, if we're lucky, a new investor comes in with the cash, boots us out, and picks up our pieces. And assumes our liabilities. More likely, she doesn't. More likely we close our doors and slip off into the night, that second mortgage looming darkly on our horizon, with nothing to water ski behind on Sunday afternoon.

The moral?

Never, never, never start up a business until the financing is in place.

If there was a more forceful way to make the point, I'd use it.

So where do we begin in our quest for cash?

If the numbers are big enough, the story sexy enough, and the entrepreneur's skin tough enough, there is always the public marketplace. None of the above ever applied to me. I'm as private as private can be (see chapter 43).

My first stop was always the bank, especially if my personal and business balance sheets (how those bankers love fat balance sheets) were of sufficient strength to satisfy their conservative demands. Conservative demands that are getting more conservative every day, at the expense of the little guy. We no longer are the customer in the banking equation. Be prepared for arched eyebrows and furrowed foreheads. Rejection is no longer for sales-people alone.

However, entrepreneurial opinion to the contrary, there are bankers out there who are creative and understanding, capable of sorting out the good plans from the bad. If our plan is good enough, and if we are good enough, there is a banker somewhere who will listen. It's up to us to find him.

Don't overlook the out-of-town banks with commercial offices in your hometown. They are usually hungrier than the local lenders and often will do deals that the hometown keepers of the cash won't touch. Minneapolis's three biggest banks wouldn't give me the time of day as we went through our whirlwind of growth in the mideighties, but two out-of-town banks, one from Boston and one from New York, were beating my doors down.

Feel free to try the venture capitalists, if your story is sexy enough and their assistance and guidance and hands-on management style are digestible. But be prepared for more interference and pressure than many of us can handle. Cash is not the only working asset we get when we do our deals with them. They are buying equity, not debt, and they want to be on the playing field, as opposed to watching from the sidelines. They expect to be heard and seen. Often. And be sure that the specter of going public sometime in the future is within your threshold of acceptability. It's their favorite way to get paid.

Venture capitalists, unlike bankers, are not hung up on fat balance sheets. They look first at the players and then at the niche, followed immediately by the size of the opportunity. And if you're asking for less than a million, you're wasting their time. The upside potential isn't there.

Financing six-figure deals is the most difficult task and comes with the fewest options. The potatoes are too small for the venture folks, as well as for the capital formation markets. If our personal balance sheets won't do the trick at the bank, it is time to turn to friends, relatives, or angels.

If you are like me, it takes unswerving confidence in your story and in yourself, along with a bellyful of intestinal fortitude, to ask friends and relatives for cash. OK, so I'm not too proud, and I've done it before, but it ranks right up there in level of discomfort with hernia operations. The possibility of losing the savings of family or friends is significantly more frightening than losing your own.

Angels are the most elusive option but also the best. Angels, in their purest form, are rich folks who have money they can lend or invest, and who are experienced enough to understand and live with the risks they take. Some are hands-on professionals, some hands-off amateurs. There are no rules governing an angel's behavior—almost anything goes. There are no angel organizations regurgitating rules and regulations. Their motives may vary. Some are intent on increasing their net worth, some do their deals because they want to help deserving entrepreneurs, others are looking to satisfy insatiable egos. Some angels fly in flocks, some solo. Some look for equity, others for debt.

Angels are like the highway patrol. We know they're around but can never seem to find them when they're needed. They maintain understandably low profiles. Finding an angel requires persistence, a black book with a wealth of networking contacts, a clean reputation, and more than a little luck. But somewhere within the framework of our acquaintances is a banker, an accountant, a lawyer, a business broker, a friend, or someone within our industry who knows where to find an angel.

There is in my home state, for instance, a low-profile, not-for-profit, entrepreneur-angel matchmaking agency called the Minnesota Cooperation Office. Unfortunately, I never knew it existed until it was too late.

I once needed $300,000 to get National Screenprint through another holiday crunch. Thanks to a friendly banker's tip, I found my designated angel hovering between deals. He poked and prodded under my company's hood on his one and only visit. The questions he asked were designed to probe inside me more than into my business. He looked deeper into my eyes than into our financial statements.

He departed after a one-hour meeting with a noncommittal good-bye, then called the next day and suggested I stop by and pick up a check for $300,000. He charged us 4 percent over prime for four months, by far the easiest deal I ever made. No equity, no meddling, no lawyers.

Lucky? Perhaps. But I did some digging in advance, maintained a network of potential resources, kept my skirts clean, and wasn't afraid to ask for the order, as our salespeople are trained to do.

The Small Business Administration is also reluctantly in the business of lending money. They cannot, however, or so they say, generate a loan unless all other public and private options have been investigated and are closed. As might be expected, cutting through their red tape is a laborious procedure. They consider themselves to be, rightfully, a lender of last resort.

There are also seed-capital funds, especially for those start-ups that are technology based. Seed-capital funds have been created by state and local governments to generate jobs and growth within their geographical borders. (Contact the National Business Incubations Association, 1 President Street, Athens, Ohio 45701.)

By and large, a well-prepared business plan in the hands of a capable entrepreneur will eventually get matched up with a lender or investor. The matching process requires aggressiveness, perseverance, and a lot of the entrepreneur's time, but aren't these the same traits we will need to survive in the business world anyway?

In the final analysis, the degree of difficulty encountered in the capital formation process is nature's way of sorting out the doers from the dreamers. Those wannabe entrepreneurs who either cannot sell their dreams or don't have the energy and the commitment to pursue them to consummation should best pursue other less demanding endeavors.

The system is teaching us an early lesson. Better to learn it now than later.

## THE BOTTOM LINE

The financing process is the most unpredictable and chancy task the entrepreneur performs as he attempts to piece together the various components of the emerging business. He has the fewest options to pursue and the least control over the results.

Locating financing is difficult and time-consuming, but good preparation for the tribulations of running a business, a pastime that also tests perseverance and tenacity.

Oh, yes. Be sure to get enough capital the first time around. There may not be a second chance.

# 9

---

# DETAILS

---

THE TASKS THAT we must perform as we assemble the pieces of our start-up can be divided into two categories: 1) those that we enjoy, and 2) those that we don't.

A partial list of those that we enjoy includes:

1. Developing the business plan and related strategies
2. All tasks related to sales, distribution, and marketing
3. Product development
4. The hiring and assembly of the management and sales teams
5. Agreements with vendors and suppliers
6. Financing (OK, maybe we don't enjoy it, but by now, we know damn well we have to do it)
7. Acquiring the physical plant and equipment

There is little need to worry about the items on this list getting done properly and on time. Common sense and our enthusiasm will see to that.

Those that we don't enjoy? Just about everything else.

Here are several tips on how we can save the down-the-road

headaches that are sure to result from putting off those details we don't enjoy:

**1. Do it yourself the first time around.** Don't delegate any of those initial tasks that will show up as recurring expense items on the P&L, no matter how painful they are to perform initially. Make sure they are done right the first time. Avoid getting locked into long-term contracts, leases, or agreements that could later restrict your growth or alter your exit options.

If it means dollars, it's your job the first time. You can always designate the maintenance after you've set it up.

**2. Insurance.** Show me somebody who likes insurance and I'll show you somebody who isn't an entrepreneur at heart. It's a damnable expense that never goes away, inflates every year, and is impossible to zero-base. (Besides, it's boring.) Don't entrust this category to anyone else until you're sure you've got what you need.

**3. Workmen's comp.** Absolutely the most frustrating expense on the P&L. In some states this category is responsible for driving otherwise capable entrepreneurs out of their minds, out of their state, and out of their business. Shop around for a trustworthy insurance guru, make him a friend, meet with him and a representative of the state, and learn how to keep the experience ratio at a minimum. High experience ratios are ultimate bottom-line hits and take light-years to correct.

**4. The lease.** Reading leases is for lawyers. Pay them their two hundred bucks, and make sure what you see is what you get. And don't get locked into long-term leases by the lure of early free rent. You'll live to regret it.

**5. Employee records.** Establish and maintain a thorough record on every employee and record the individual employment agreements reached with each of them. Make two copies, one for the files and one for the employee. Keep a running written record of any commendations or reprimands during the time of employment. I guarantee these written records will be used more than once to save your skin.

**6. Recording your deals.** The typical entrepreneur's business deals, big and small, are creative and complex and subject to memory lapses unless written down. Putting them on paper is time-consuming but do it anyway, whether with employees, shareholders, debtors, customers, or vendors. Get guidelines from an attorney before cutting the important and most creative deals, and no matter what you negotiate with shareholders, run it by an attorney first. Those shareholder deals that appear minuscule today will grow to life-size proportions some time in the future. Guaranteed.

**7. Licenses—city, state, and federal.** Visit similar businesses in the area and find out what is needed. Putting this off will only trigger fines as well as double the time it takes to get it done later.

**8. Signing of checks.** Do it yourself until such time as you a) have a complete understanding of the check-producing procedure; b) have a feel for your recurring expenses; and c) can turn the responsibility over to someone you absolutely, positively trust.

Think about it. How can you be too busy to disburse your scarce cash?

**9. When in doubt, use an attorney.** In a perfect world, attorneys would be required to do constructive work, like the rest of the population. This is not a perfect world. Use them. Much of what they do, even at their inflated hourly fees, will save headaches and cash down the road.

There is a host of equally aggravating and minute details in addition to those listed above. These happen to be the most unenjoyable I can remember putting off.

## THE BOTTOM LINE

There is a long list of details that the start-up entrepreneur must perform. Responsibility for the accomplishment of this list should not be delegated the first time around.

Today's postponed details turn into tomorrow's major headaches. Worse, the postponement establishes a culture of procrastination in the fledgling company.

# III

# THE INSIDE
# PLAYERS

# 10

## PRODUCT
## CHAMPION

THERE ARE TWO kinds of mousetraps, those that are products and those that are junk.

Garages the world over are littered with mousetraps that will never reach the retailer's shelves. Twentieth-century mousetraps they well may be, computerized and solar-powered and lighter than air. Inexpensive mousetraps, too, capable of catching more mice faster than anything available for purchase today.

Meanwhile, those mousetraps that are on the retailer's shelves, available to consumers, are successful products. Inferior, perhaps, to those relegated to the garage but plugged into the system nonetheless.

There is no universal economic law that says only the best products must reach the marketplace. Making the best product, as many starving inventors can attest, is but one ingredient (and not the primary one at that) of the multifaceted business stew.

That stew has many chefs. The inventor, the manufacturer, the salesperson, the marketer, and legions of administrators are all a part of the process, as the product winds from inception to shelves.

Standing over that stew, stirring and blending the ingredients, is the product champion. The adoring parent. The instigator, the believer, the fire-eating doer who takes that mousetrap and somehow muscles it onto somebody's shelves.

It is the product champion who senses consumer appeal. It is the product champion who positions, alters, and massages the product to fit his perception of what the market wants. If he's right, the widget takes off; if he's wrong, it crashes. He designs the distribution, always the most important component of the path to the marketplace. He studies the competition and traces the product's successes and failures, and does not rest until all of the stew's ingredients are blended to his taste. Any product champion worth his salt is not satisfied until the product has achieved his own lofty goals, not someone else's.

In the world of the Fortune 500, product champions are usually the sales and marketing types—those folks with an understanding of such murky subjects as advertising, market share, and consumer tastes.

In our small, entrepreneurial companies, we are usually the product champions. (In the beginning, who else is there?) We take our version of the mousetrap, embellish it, package it, and bundle it off to the marketplace, between signing checks and opening the mail. Like everything else, we learn the all-important marketing and distribution lessons at the hands of that unfriendly mentor, trial and error.

If we want our product to succeed badly enough, it usually does. If we aren't willing to pay the price, it won't. Perseverance pays big dividends in the product champion business.

But the time will come, as our company matures, when our role as product champion must be passed on to others. Playing fields change, players change, we change. The mantle may be passed to a sales manager, a marketing manager, an assistant, or a protégé. To someone who will adopt our enthusiasm for the product and is in a position to infect others with it. To someone who will listen to our customers. To someone who understands our industry's product-to-market equation and can match distribution with customer needs. To someone who will take the success of the product personally, as we once did, and will persevere until his personal goals are achieved.

So how do you know a product champion when you see one?

Look for a bulldog. A creative, fast-moving, nonstop, hell-bent-for-leather bulldog. An often unreasonable bulldog who nudges, pushes, and steamrolls whatever it is that is blocking the product's path to the marketplace. A believer in the product, often to the point of irrationality. A perseverer against all odds.

You'll know those bulldogs because they are often found agitating the people around them, particularly those who are into numbers and rational thinking. Nor are bulldogs in any danger of endearing themselves to those who don't share their vision. There is no middle ground when dealing with product champions. You're on their team or you're not. It's their way or the highway.

And their way is usually the right way—at least where the product is concerned.

We may choose, when our own reign as product champion ends, to move up, move down, or move on. Move up to full-time management, God forbid, or move down to the laboratory where the whole thing started, or move on to another start-up, if we have the energy and it's still in our blood.

Whatever choice we make, it is our responsibility to assure that a new product champion is firmly anchored in place before we go. A bulldog who won't rest until that product is churning and selling and finding a shelf to fill.

By itself, our product is only an invention. Nothing more.

## THE BOTTOM LINE

Every successful company must have a product champion, pushing and pulling, making things happen.

The product champion is usually the entrepreneur at the early stages of growth. In later years, when his attention is spread too thin, it will be his responsibility to ensure there is a product champion in the wings, ready to bulldog, persevering where the entrepreneur left off.

# 11

## FINANCIAL

## PERSON

YOU HEARD IT here, if you haven't heard it before.

The most important hire you will ever make is your financial person.

Financial people—bookkeepers, controllers, and CFOs—will never make us, but they can damn well break us. Or stand idly by as we break ourselves. A good financial person will give us the latitude to spend our time doing those things we like to do, the things we do best. A weak one will usurp our time and waste our energy and otherwise find ways to make our lives unproductive.

Financial folks aren't that big a deal, you say? Take a look at their imposing list of responsibilities:

### THE FINANCIAL PERSON

- Manages assets, including cash.
- Tracks and controls expenses.
- Prepares budgets and forecasts.
- Supervises management information systems. "If you can't measure it you can't manage it," the saying goes, and it is up to the financial person to provide those measurements.

- Manages accounting department personnel.
- Produces accurate, timely, user-friendly financial statements.
- Takes care of all corporate taxes, and ensures that their effects on the entrepreneur's personal affairs are considered.
- Maintains banking relationships.
- Oversees many of those human resource issues that have nowhere else to go (until the company can afford to hire a human resources person).
- Makes, and keeps, the entrepreneur computer friendly.
- Is an integral member of the After Five O'Clock Club— the unofficial committee that meets in the office after the workday and on Saturday mornings to determine the fate of the company.
- Is usually the designated rein-puller and in-house devil's advocate.

Let's face it, we entrepreneurs don't want to spend our time balancing checkbooks. (If we did, we wouldn't be entrepreneurs.) Nor do we have any burning desire to count inventory, shop for office supply discounts, or chase deadbeats and slowpays.

We're too busy assembling our team, managing them, and making things happen. Or we should be, anyway.

Here is some hard-earned advice on hiring your first, next, and hopefully last financial person—from a shell-shocked veteran who hired three in ten years. And should have hired four. But would have been better off hiring only one.

The financial candidate must be able to:

1. Solve today's problems. (They usually can.)

2. Anticipate tomorrow's problems. (Not as easy.)

3. Assemble and manage a staff capable of performing the long list of duties described above.

4. Relate to, and communicate with, all departments of the company—including sales. (This doesn't mean the financial person must always agree with sales, only that he can discuss issues without losing his objectivity. And his temper.)

**5.** Have a keen sense of timeliness. Numbers are important, but they must be fresh to be relevant. (For instance, unaudited month-end reports should be out not later than the 15th of the following month.)

I hired my first financial person at the outset of our Sunshine Years. He dangled a Big Eight background and an impressive pedigree in my anxious face, and I bit. It turned out he was a whiz at solving today's problems and adequate at anticipating tomorrow's, and he questioned every penny we spent. Every penny.

But he couldn't talk to our salespeople. I mean he couldn't even *talk*. His mouth would move, but words wouldn't come out. Nor could they talk to him. That cold war unfolded every day with me in the middle.

Characteristically, I overreacted. My next two financial hires were the mellowest, friendliest CPA types I could find. Harmony and goodwill reigned throughout the company. Our salespeople thought they had died and gone to heaven, while our systems died and went to hell.

Financial people, the proven ones at least, do not come cheap. Since most $5-million-a-year companies can't afford $100,000 CFOs, an emerging one is needed. Someone with untapped talent.

How do you find that emerger? Damned if I know, because I never could. But in the process of trying, I've learned a few rules about hiring CFOs:

**1.** Recognize going in that the CFO (or controller) hire is absolutely, positively, the most important one you will ever make. The time-consuming and nitpicking interview process must be strictly adhered to.

**2.** Make this hiring number one on the To Do list, and leave it on the top until completed.

**3.** Don't rush it. Take your time. It is far better to miss out on a good hire than it is to make a bad one.

**4.** Maximize due diligence when checking references. Interviewing CFOs can be boring stuff, but if there's a skeleton in the candidate's closet, it needs to be found now, not later. (See chapter 32.)

**5.** The financial person's communication skills are as important as his technical skills. Don't be swayed by the number-spouter unless he can communicate.

**6.** Make sure that the candidate understands and accepts responsibility for the wide range of CFO responsibilities. Review the list of responsibilities before you make the offer.

**7.** Hire a CPA as soon as you can afford one. The comfort level of your bankers and vendors will increase proportionally.

**8.** It is often difficult for the interviewing entrepreneur to determine a CPA's technical competence. Ask your accountant to interview the narrowed-down choices and give a professional opinion.

**9.** Use your existing network to locate candidates. Inquire of accountants, attorneys, vendors, and friends. Word of mouth is always the best resource.

**10.** Don't pinch pennies in the process. There are plenty of headhunters around specializing in accounting and financial types.

Financial candidates abound. Run an ad and watch the mail overflow with a torrent of gleaming résumés. Temporary and permanent financial people are available to rent or to buy. Most friends and business acquaintances have at least one juicy financial candidate stashed away somewhere, awaiting an opportunity exactly like yours.

Financial candidates are a commodity.

Good hires are not.

### THE BOTTOM LINE

The financial person can make the entrepreneur's life enjoyable. Or miserable. The entrepreneur has only himself to blame if it's the latter. He hired him. And procrastinated when the time came to fire him.

The best financial people are the ones who grow up with the company.

Hire for tomorrow, not for today.

# 12

## SOMEONE TO PICK UP
## THE PIECES

*"Give me a crowbar and a place to stand, and I can move the world."*

—Anonymous Pantser

AND SO GOES our cry in those early Phase I days, as we greet the UPS driver, open the mail, and sweep the warehouse floor. We can and do move the world on our broad but aching shoulders, combining sweat and desire to get the job done. We don't need a lot of assistance in those early days.

There will come a time, however, when sweat and desire are no longer enough. About the time we graduate from pantser to entrepreneur. About the time the bookkeeper is replaced by an honest-to-God controller ˙or CFO. About the time the long-awaited Sunshine Years cast their welcome light over our company and our life.

As the list of our responsibilities lengthens, we leave a cluttered trail wherever we pass. The trail includes a vast array of half-finished projects, forgotten needs, and overlooked details. Along with a slew of unresolved problems, jobs to be finished, calls to be followed up, and fences to be mended.

Yes, the day will finally come when we run out of time. Or out of tricks in our organizational bag. Those discarded details accumulate and are left unattended and soon forgotten. We need help—someone to follow behind us, completing our half-finished projects, wrapping up our partially resolved problems. Someone to work in our wake and act in our absence. Not a gofer, but someone who gives as much of a damn as we do. Someone who has a scent of the dream.

This someone could be the financial person, or perhaps an operations employee if the financial person isn't heavy enough. Or doesn't want the job. This someone could be an office manager or maybe a secretary. Even a spouse.

Left to their own devices, the forgotten details will accumulate, leaving a legacy of junk and confusion as the Sunshine Years run their inevitable course—a legacy that will only shorten those enjoyable years and hasten the approach of the Years from Hell.

For our sanity and our company's safety, someone must follow behind us and pick up the pieces. His reward is lifelong employment and a role in fulfilling our dream. The reward for our company is exemption from the clutter we leave behind.

The reward for the entrepreneur is peace of mind and the freedom to move forward without having to look back.

## THE BOTTOM LINE

Details don't get resolved by themselves. Or by the entrepreneur, who should have something better to do with his time.

If the entrepreneur is to find the time and energy to perform those tasks that are a part of his job description, he needs someone to follow his trail.

Left alone, a string of forgotten details will send the company on a detour to trouble. An expressway to the Years from Hell.

# IV

## THE OUTSIDE
## PLAYERS

# 13

## MENTORS

THERE ARE ONLY three things I know for sure about mentors: 1) I never had one; 2) I wish I had; and 3) the next time around I certainly will.

Think about it. Our counterparts in the corporate world have been exposed to countless hours of formal and informal training, from within and without. They attended seminars and classes, read manuals and directives, and grew up in mature organizations that went to endless pains to take trial and error out of the average stiff's workday. Unlike the majority of us entrepreneurs, the corporate guy's formal education did not come to a halt after graduation from high school or college.

The corporate trainee also had twenty lean and hungry entry-level friends just down the hall, all cut from the same I-can't-get-there-fast-enough mold. All were similarly trained, educated, focused, and hungry. They were placed on organized and defined career paths. They interfaced by the day, hour, minute, learning from the successes and failures of somebody other than themselves.

As if that isn't enough, many had mentors as their careers progressed. Those mentors would teach, and lead, and in many ways help them to eliminate trial and error as a management tool. They also were there to set examples, inspire, and even kick butt when required. (Something most of us could use now and again.)

Meanwhile, back in our cluttered offices, we entrepreneurs spend the better part of our lives jousting with a thousand unyielding windmills, wearing the same rusty armor and riding the same aging steed as our predecessors. And our peers down the street.

Oh, we have our mentors—and jim-dandies they are too. Mr. Trial and Ms. Error are our faithful teachers. Their style is ancient and basic. If it works, move on. If it doesn't, regroup. Start over at square one.

Simple, inefficient, time-consuming. And dumb.

Bankers, accountants, friends, and even UPS drivers chip in when they can, as they do their best to take the place of mentors in our lives. They feed us tasty morsels from the scraps of their own kitchens, but we never get close to the main course. To understand, you have to have been where we're going. Let's face it, they haven't.

Our crusty independence, often the wind behind our sails, doubles as the anchor impeding our progress. We are alone, and too often remain alone, in a vocation where progress can be abetted by the addition of experience.

Somewhere out there is a wise and grizzled ex-entrepreneur who may spare an hour or two a week to work with us. We should network our friends, accountants, bankers, lawyers, and vendors to find him. We should give him whatever he wants in exchange for his help. His price could not rival what we will eventually pay in trial-and-error tuition.

Here are a few tips on how to work with mentors:

**1.** Mentoring is a personal experience. If the chemistry is right, the mentoring process will work. If it isn't, it won't. Get to know your mentor before you fall in bed with him.

**2.** The best way to keep a mentor? Listen to him. Keep an open mind when he speaks. Follow up on his suggestions. Give him constant feedback on what works and what doesn't. Like anybody else, mentors need to feel they are contributing.

**3.** The best way to get rid of a mentor? Ask him for money to put into the business. (If he's interested, let him bring it up. Otherwise, leave him alone.)

**4.** Don't be protective toward mentors. They need to know what your problems are. Remember, they've been there before. They know what's going on behind the scenes when you don't tell it like it is. Be truthful with a mentor, or be history with him.

**5.** The better the mentor, the more questions he will ask, and the more questions he asks, the tougher they become. Be ready for the barrage, and don't be overly sensitive.

Good mentors can tell us what will work and what won't, without our having to learn the hard way. They can show us where to go and where not to go, and what to do once we get there.

Listen to your mentor, and weigh the choices he presents. Confer and discuss with him. Then make decisions based on his experience and on the confidence of knowing that two heads are infinitely better than one.

Leave trial and error to competitors. It's too expensive for us.

## THE BOTTOM LINE

If I had it to do over again, I would find a mentor before I wrote a business plan.

# 14

---

## BANKERS

---

I DON'T DISLIKE bankers. Neither do I understand them.

They loan zillions to will-o'-the-wisp Latin American governments. Billions to Milken-like paper shufflers. Millions to Trump-like real estate jugglers. And they don't understand why they never get paid.

Then they turn around and beat up us little folks when our car payments are late.

There's one other thing I don't understand about bankers. They have this long-distance vision problem. The further away the customers, the better they appear. The Minneapolis banks wouldn't touch my company in the early 1980s. Meanwhile, the big boys from Boston and New York duked it out over the rights to our meager balance sheet.

I'd bet my favorite sweatshirt that had my company been based in New York, the Minneapolis banks would have sent limousines to our door. While the Boston and New York folks scoured the Midwest for a screenprinting company.

See? I just don't understand them.

I'm not saying that bankers are always wrong. The perception of their shortcomings in the eyes of entrepreneurs might have something to do with our jaundiced point of view. It is unfathomable, for instance, how any sane human being could not be in awe of our business plan and of us, dressed in a new pinstripe suit, as we make our silken pitch. How can they not be intrigued, we wonder, by our solid niche, our professional presentation, our impeccable management team, and our impressive financial projections for the year 2010 and beyond?

But if we have been told no by a dozen bankers, then the possibility exists that something might be wrong with the deal. Our plan may be too vague, our team too unpedigreed, our venture too fuzzy. God knows they've seen and heard it all. And been burned by it all, especially in the late 1980s.

Most bankers aren't dummies. They know that the entrepreneurial odds are heavily—make that overwhelmingly—stacked against us. They read the obits.

OK, so maybe most bankers are conservative, uncreative, lacking in business moxie, and professional naysayers. But if they weren't, they wouldn't be bankers. They're bred for their careers, just like we are. If they said yes to every deal that passed over their desks, there wouldn't be enough cash in their vaults to fund a lemonade stand. Which is about where we stand today, given the excesses of the past decade.

One on one, bankers can be pleasant. But, like children and dogs, put them in a pack (or a committee) and they become downright dangerous.

I remember the first time I encountered a committee of bankers. The year was 1972, two years after the First National Bank of Minneapolis had somehow overlooked my paltry personal balance sheet and helped me finance the purchase of a small sporting goods company. The relationship between Minneapolis's biggest bank and its scrawniest entrepreneur proceeded smoothly for several years, thanks to our profitable operations and a hands-on, capable account executive who serviced our account. He knew everything that went on in my company, good or bad. I saw to that.

One day that account executive, now a friend, stopped by to pass on the news that my loan application must now be approved by "the committee," because our borrowing needs had passed some magic dollar level. This new procedure was only a formality, he assured me. There was nothing to worry about.

*The committee!* He may as well have said the tribunal. The KGB. My life and the fate of my company were now in the hands of the committee! Three guys named Joe.

A year or so later the inevitable happened. "The committee regrets to inform you," the voice on the phone began. With the word "regrets" I went into a lack-of-financial-security oxygen deficiency. My vision blurred and my hearing faded. I remember little of the remainder of that conversation, including the reason for our disqualification.

I eventually survived, thanks to a small neighborhood bank. And I've learned to live with committees of bankers over the years. But I still don't trust them. Never will.

You say you have a banker you like? Here are a few suggestions on how to keep him:

**1.** Remember, the customer/vendor equation is no longer at work in this relationship. Today, the entrepreneur needs the banker one hell of a lot more than the banker needs the entrepreneur. There will be, for the foreseeable future at least, more demand for his product than there is supply. Swallow your ego, and treat him like the customer.

**2.** Call him more often than he calls you. Not just with the good news; call him with the bad. He doesn't like yesterday's negative surprises any more than you do. Can you blame him?

How often should you call him? Whenever there is news that will interest him, good or bad. Every two months, two weeks, or two days, whatever it takes.

You can't call your banker too often. You can call him too infrequently.

**3.** Always ask for more money than you think you need. A little insurance never hurt anybody, and you usually won't get everything you ask for, anyway. Besides, there's nothing worse than having to go back to the well the second time.

**4.** When he visits, remember, it isn't a social call he's paying, no matter what he says. He's kicking the tires. Prepare well in advance for each of his visits: formal agenda, outline, and tour.

He should take notes on the presentation, ask his questions, and make a record of his visit on the outline you provide. The next day follow up the meeting with a letter recapping the issues discussed and the decisions reached.

Help the guy do his job. He won't complain. See that he gets more than he asks for when he visits. Undercommit and overdeliver, as you should be doing for your customers. Your banker will go away happy, his boss will stay away happy, and you will breathe easier. Until his next visit, anyway.

**5.** Nobody in his right mind wants to guarantee anything. But if you want what your banker has, chances are you're going to have to do some guaranteeing. (Think about it, if you were in his shoes, wouldn't you ask for the same?)

There are several kinds of guarantees (unlimited, limited, joint and several, and time). Check with an attorney before signing one. And remember, guarantees are forever, unless stated otherwise. Keep a record of everything guaranteed, be it with a bank or a vendor. You never can tell when an old guarantee will come back to haunt you.

**6.** Bankers may sneak a peek at financial projections ten years out, but only when they have nothing better to do. Save yourself the trouble. Five years of projections is more than enough.

**7.** Bankers are making loans, not equity injections. Thus they want to know everything about the company's assets—inventory, receivables, equipment, real estate. They need to understand exactly how those assets can be converted into cash when, and if, the bad times roll.

Meanwhile, the entrepreneur views the world through rose-colored glasses. Failure is not in his crystal ball. Understand the difference between these two viewpoints and help the banker do his job.

**8.** Financial performance and the resultant changes on the balance sheet can be reasons to change the terms of a loan in midstream. Don't be surprised if rates go up when times are tough and the bank's risk increases.

Oh yes, that stream flows both ways. So don't be afraid to ask for better terms as the balance sheet strengthens and the bank's risk decreases.

My banker, during our busy season, had five or six times more cash tied up in my company than I did. Is it any wonder he wanted to know why I canned our latest CFO or closed the Chicago office? Why 15 percent of our receivables were over 90 days or our inventory only turned three times last year?

Bankers are a fact of life. Learn to live with them, or face a worse fate.

Shareholders.

## THE BOTTOM LINE

Bankers are bred to be skeptical. Understand where they are coming from and learn to anticipate their questions and reactions.

Prepare thoroughly for bankers when they visit. Avoid surprises. Help make their job easier.

In the 1980s bankers looked at the P&L first. In the 1990s they'll head directly for the balance sheet.

If you are opposed to providing personal guarantees, find another career.

# 15

## LAWYERS

I HAVE A close friend who is a lawyer. A good one, too; he has ably defended my turf more than once. But in those elbows-on-the-table-over-a-few-beers conversations that occur too infrequently between friends, he has confided that he is not entirely content, lawyering his life away.

After all, it is conflict he sells, and solutions to conflict. If he does his job well, he enhances his client's life. Meanwhile, across the table, the party of the second part takes it on the chin. Winners beget losers in his litigious world. There cannot be one without the other.

Making matters worse, thanks to a flawed judicial system, his winners don't always deserve to win, or his losers to lose. These are high-stakes games he plays with his customers' lives.

My friend would trade his profession for mine, or a facsimile thereof, in a microsecond. In the world of the entrepreneur, we perform our role dutifully, and what happens? A new product or service creates new sales, new customers, new jobs and opportunities for everybody. Everybody can walk home a winner in the games we play—there need be no losers.

Meanwhile, half of the time my lawyer friend is losing, while the other half his opponent is losing. Every day.

I suspect that the declining American perception of the practice of law began ten or fifteen years ago. Somewhere around the time the number of lawyers exceeded the quantity needed to carry on our daily business. Legions of freshly trained lawyers had to create, or search out, new conflicts. The old conflicts, those that come naturally to us imperfect human beings, were no longer sufficient to satisfy the never-ending swarm.

Thus lawyers became purveyors of conflict. Law firms hired ad agencies and hit the media with their message to the downtrodden. We listened, nodded our heads that we were being transgressed against by an unholy alliance of neighbors, bosses, relatives, and friends. Lo and behold, a whole new set of outrageous conflicts was born. The race was on.

This flood of lawyers in the marketplace has touched us all. Lawyers used to be like FBI agents: the average person on the street was aware they existed, and sometimes we even met one, but we never had occasion to deal with one. They practiced their trade on someone else. Never on us.

Today lawyers are like pets. Everybody has one.

If I worked for General Motors, lawyers would be fellow employees, lost in the overhead shuffle like everybody else. A fixed expense, like rent and sales meetings and the CEO's limousine driver.

But I don't work for GM. To me, lawyers are an unnecessary expense: bottom-line profits gone awry, a capital expenditure that must wait for another year, a new employee on hold. Additionally, lawyers are user unfriendly—consulting with them takes time away from work and results in lost efficiency on the job.

Sooner or later, however, all of us must come face to face with a lawyer. It's the American way. When it occurs, here are several suggestions on how to cut the losses:

1. When it is absolutely, positively necessary to find a lawyer, don't shop price. Shop quality. Like with cars and quarterbacks, there is a huge difference in quality, and that difference usually translates into winning or losing.

**2.** Find a contemporary lawyer, one who knows the difference between customers and clients. Yesterday's lawyers talk down their noses to clients, today's lawyers talk across the table to customers. It doesn't take long to sense the difference.

**3.** Get an estimate of their hourly fees and the total tab in advance. It won't hold up, but they will know you're watching and that you will ask them to justify any increases.

**4.** Make lawyers itemize their bills. Your customers don't accept lump-sum invoices for your product, and neither should you.

**5.** Don't let them chat; their meters are always running.

**6.** Lawyers are not always right, no matter how imposing they may appear. Their profession is gray. The power of logic, theirs and yours, working in unison with their knowledge of the law, plays a significant role in success or failure. Laymen are capable of logic, too. Feel free to use it in their presence.

**7.** Pay lawyers in sixty days, and don't bounce the check. They make formidable enemies.

**8.** Raise your children to be entrepreneurs.

There is, unfortunately, a time and a place for lawyers in the entrepreneur's environment. Despite the pain of exchanging much-needed cash for legal fees, this book is sprinkled with recommendations on occasions when lawyers should be consulted.

An ounce of prevention is still worth a pound of cure.

## THE BOTTOM LINE

The best advice regarding lawyers: Avoid them. When you can't, get the best. And when they don't deliver, fire them.

Deal with lawyers the way you would with any other vendor in an industry where supply exceeds demand. Get quotes and itemized invoices and expect to be treated like a customer.

And finally, beware of those folks, friends and foes alike, who refer to lawyers as counsel, and who retain more than one law firm. They are the veterans.

# 16

## ACCOUNTANTS

SHOW ME AN honest and reasonably profitable entrepreneur, and I'll show you a person who almost looks forward to seeing the accountants every year.

I'm not saying it's a warm and gratifying feeling writing the bean counters their checks for services rendered. They don't work for peanuts, and anything that doesn't go into Cost of Goods Sold hurts.

Accountants are, however, when all is said and done, the keepers of the ultimate score, and that score is one of the primary reasons we play the ultimate game. Where our motives are something other than the ultimate score, the bean counters still give us the legitimacy and credibility we need to maintain our financing from lenders, vendors, and (when all else fails) shareholders.

Most accountants, unlike their attorney counterparts, know and respect the difference between a customer and a client. Today's accountants are trained to lead us through the endless maze of government rules and regulations and still make us feel like customers in the process. They have learned to talk with us, not at us.

This responsiveness to customers on the part of the accounting profession has more than a little relevance to the degree of competition in their industry. There is at least one accountant on every streetcorner, and the successful ones recognize that they are offering their customers a service, not granting them a privilege. They are, like the rest of us, in the relationship-building business.

Accountants come in three distinct packages: the small Smith and Cratchits, the midsize regionals, and the Big Six—the imposing nationals.

I patronized the Smith and Cratchits during my early pantser years. I'd do so again at that stage of my business career, because their meters run at a quasi-reasonable rate. (The Big Six and most regionals don't want our peanutlike business anyway, no matter what they say.) The Smith and Cratchits can provide all of the services that most of us need at that stage of our growth, and our business matters to them.

I ultimately switched to one of the nationals, not so much by choice as by necessity. My creditors, vendors and banks alike, collectively demanded the gilded Big Six signature on my financial statements, seeking the comfort of their expertise and the depth of their pockets as our credit lines continued to grow.

An additional benefit of working with the nationals is the wide array of services they are capable of bringing to the entrepreneurial table. Most of them come armed with a stockpile of experts anxiously waiting in the wings to assist us with our MIS, inventory, receivables, tax, cash flow, and even personnel problems.

Unfortunately, the nationals are to the accounting profession what Bloomingdale's is to the retail trade. We are not talking K Mart's everyday low pricing here. Someone must pay for their marble foyers, prestigious addresses, and stockpiled consultants. That someone is the customer. Be prepared.

*Accounting Today* magazine provides a ready example of this disparity in the cost of hiring an accountant. They cite the hourly partner rates in New York City:

| | |
|---|---|
| Big Six | $235 |
| Regional | $150 |

| | |
|---|---|
| Medium Local | $142 |
| Small Local | $117 |

The nationals also have an inflated idea of the degree to which they can relate to us small business folks. Fortune 500 in size themselves, their favorite customers have similar girth and their environment works against them when they attempt to relate to us little people. They do their best to tune in, but there are too many decades of inbred organizational genes.

The accounting profession in general, and the nationals in particular, provide one useful service that comes without an invoice. Accountants can be an efficient networking resource for many of our management needs.

Looking for a CFO, controller, or even a president? Accountants, and especially the nationals, are a regular underground employment agency. Their far-flung tentacles reach everywhere throughout the local (and sometimes national) business community.

Accountants can also provide a unique perspective on our business that is unavailable from any other outside resource. Early in my entrepreneurial career I learned a valuable lesson on viewpoint from mine.

"Happy with your results?" my accountant asked, as we reviewed our year-end financials.

"Of course," I gloated, in my supreme ignorance. "Our ROS was five percent, our ROE twelve percent. Maybe those figures won't measure up to Microsoft, but they're better than the average small business."

"And what about your ROA?" he asked, obviously unimpressed. "Are you happy with that?"

"Uh, well, we don't focus on ROA."

"Jim, your ROA was four percent. With that kind of a return on assets you may as well buy treasury bonds and go practice your putting," he yawned. Tact was never his forte.

He went on to explain that, because we were highly leveraged, we could have decent returns on sales and equity and still have a piddly return on our assets. From that day forward we shifted our financial focus to ROA.

A few tips on the subject of accountants:

**1.** Select an accountant the same way you hire an employee. Interview more than one, check their references, and kick the hell out of their tires. Word-of-mouth referrals are always the best (lawyers and bankers are the traditional sources). Responsibility for the selection and hiring of an accountant should be shared by the entrepreneur and his financial person.

**2.** Pantsers don't need nationals—and vice versa. They're too expensive and have difficulty relating.

**3.** Most accountants, especially the Smith and Cratchits, have a niche in which they excel: manufacturing, distribution, retail, high-tech. Find a firm that is experienced in your field.

**4.** Insist upon a firm price and time quotes as part of the deal. Include a method of computing add-on services. Like lawyers' estimates, accounting quotes never hold up, but the act of quoting will help to keep the add-ons in line. And explain up front that you don't accept anything but itemized invoices.

Also, ask for a commitment as to which of the partners will handle your account, and for how long. Stability is important, and while the firm may not be able to honor the commitment, your insistence may influence their new assignment.

**5.** Pay accountants in sixty days, or even in ninety when cash is tight. They will squawk, but most will understand and have probably built the cost of the wait into their fees. They usually let the customer get by with slow pay, unless they're having cash problems of their own.

**6.** The law of supply and demand, where accountants are concerned, is tilted in the customer's direction. Use that leverage when cutting a deal or holding them to their commitments.

And don't be fooled for one minute by that Ozzie Nelson reputation of the accounting profession. It isn't so anymore. They party and play golf and entertain customers and do the same kind of things that the rest of us business folks do. Gartered sleeves, green eyeshades, and Mr. Peepers are images of the past.

Accountants are no longer professionals. Today they are businesspeople. Like us.

## THE BOTTOM LINE

Accountants, like the U.S. government, are necessary, expensive, provide a needed service, thrive on rules and regulations, and are in extreme oversupply.

Accountants have bridged the gap from professionals to businessmen. As a result, expect to be treated like a customer when dealing with them.

Accountants and accounting firms are commodities. The law of supply and demand is hard at work in their industry. Remember this when hiring. And contemplating firing.

# 17

# THE BOARD OF
# DIRECTORS

BOARDS OF DIRECTORS are like breath mints: everybody needs them, but too many of us don't partake.

Like mentors and consultants, boards of directors can provide outside perspective to us vacuum-dwelling entrepreneurs. Boards replace trial and error with experience and knowledge. They act as backboards, and feeding boards, and boards of inquiry. Boards increase our range of vision while decreasing our windows of risk. They open needed doors and close unnecessary ones. They give us a glimpse of the outside world.

Boards of directors can and will change our behavior, no minor entrepreneurial accomplishment. Previously accountable to no one, we suddenly find ourselves in a position where we are required to prepare in advance, listen, follow up, and justify yesterday's decision. We are, horror of horrors, accountable to someone. Like just about everybody else.

Boards add depth, breadth, and accountability to the entrepreneur's isolated and dictatorial world—in an ever-changing and hostile business environment where depth, breadth, and accountability are increasingly necessary for survival.

Too many entrepreneurs and most pantsers never utilize a board of directors. Excuses include:

- Too busy helping the UPS driver, opening the mail, or unloading trucks to plan board meetings.
- Board meetings require follow-up. Again, too busy.
- Good board members are hard to find. No time to look.
- Directors' insurance is too expensive.
- No outsider can tell an entrepreneur how to run his business.

The fact is, we wouldn't be so busy if we weren't correcting the mistakes we wouldn't have made, had we taken the time to solicit outside advice. And we wouldn't be so busy if we used the guidance and experience that a board of directors can provide.

A collection of tips on how to assemble and utilize a board of directors:

**1.** Directors should come from the outside, not the inside. The entrepreneur doesn't need another set of in-house heads nodding in unison at his sometimes musty ideas.

**2.** No close friends or relatives. They can't be tough enough.

**3.** Select directors from the ranks of customers, bankers, consultants, accountants, business associates, and yes, even attorneys.

**4.** Balance the board. If your strengths are sales and marketing, make sure the fields of finance and operations are covered as well. A director with experience within the industry could also help, especially if capable of viewing you through a customer's eyes.

**5.** Five directors (including you) is the absolute limit. Too many and their schedules become impossible to coordinate.

**6.** Pay them. Modestly perhaps, but pay them. Compensation makes board meetings official and assures preparation and participation.

**7.** Schedule the meetings well in advance, to fit the board members' schedules.

**8.** Send each director a thorough outline (like bankers, they don't like surprises) well in advance of the meeting, along with any reading to help them prepare.

**9.** Focus directors' meetings on strategic and overview issues, not on operations. It is important that the meetings be meaty and utilize their talents. Keep them interested.

**10.** Be open with the board. Remember, they are being paid to help resolve problems, work through issues, and set a course for the business. They are not being paid to listen to the entrepreneur pontificate, pat himself on the back, or discuss the World Series.

**11.** Use the directors' credibility. Besides advising, they can help find new customers, new vendors, and even new financing. Once they are comfortable with you and your company, get them involved.

**12.** If directors' insurance is too expensive, consider the less formal advisory board. An advisory board serves the same function as a board of directors, but the advisers are not held liable for the operation of the business. Directors, on the other hand, have fiduciary responsibility, and can be held liable for their actions. And inactions.

It is true that a board of directors introduces elements of the very environment that you were hoping to escape when you made the decision to become your own boss. But listening and following up and asking for help is not hazardous to entrepreneurial health.

And a little accountability never hurt anybody.

### THE BOTTOM LINE

A board of directors (or advisers) will bring perspective and overview to the management table, something isolated entrepreneurs can always use.

Everybody needs somebody to ask the hard questions and give the unwanted advice.

# 18

## CONSULTANTS

CONSULTANTS AND I got off to a shaky start.

I had managed to survive the first twelve years of my entrepreneurial career without the benefit of consultants and their magic wands. I ultimately weakened, and hired a retired executive type, a veteran of Minneapolis's corporate wars. He came to us packing a fistful of gold-plated references and community accomplishments.

Thanks to the fertile ground our company offered, our new consultant came out of the chutes like a newly elected mayor. The honeymoon was in full bloom that first month following his hire, and we ate hungrily from his outstretched hand. New buzzwords, fresh concepts, old experiences—he brought them all to our threadbare table. Every day was a school day for us.

Quickly determining that our new consultant was really Tom Peters in disguise, I offered him a full-time position with our company, including title, salary, bonus, and perks. A two-month unpaid winter vacation (a necessity for many of Minnesota's over-fifty set) iced the deal. He graciously accepted and quickly became a part of the team.

Another month passed, and so did the honeymoon. I had

made a megamistake. Our consultant-turned-employee had exhausted his inventory of advice that first month on the job. I mean the guy was sold out. It would be, characteristically, another six months before I, mercifully for both of us, ended it all.

**Lesson #1**: Engage a consultant as if selecting a spouse or hiring a president. Network to find one and say no to blind dates. Check those references carefully, and don't expect the average corporate career person to have much more than a clue as to what it takes to row the small business boat.

**Lesson #2**: Whatever you do, don't hand him the keys to the car before he has a license to drive.

**Lesson #3**: The ultimate cost of ineffectual consultants can only be measured in part by their fees. Add misdirection and time lost, and they are capable of running up monumental tabs in surprisingly short periods of time.

**Lesson #4**: Offer no long-term contracts. Build in a quick-exit option in the event that what you get isn't what you expected. Or what you were promised.

**Lesson #5**: Don't waste any time showing them the door when the situation demands it.

Five years later I warily hired my second consultant. Our young and relatively inexperienced sales force had grown to sixteen people, collectively clamoring, as only salespeople can, for professional training. Had I known at the time that our Years from Hell were around the corner, I would have spent those training dollars on our even younger and less experienced management staff. I didn't, however, and thus applied the grease to sales, where the squeaks were the loudest but the need the least.

This time I hired a pedigreed, professional consultant with a fistful of references in sales training. His credentials were well earned as it turned out, and the guy delivered. Too much. Our sales force greedily digested his offerings, sales exploded, and the subsequent avalanche of orders almost buried the company.

In retrospect, we would have been better off without that consultant's services. The explosion of sales kicked off and then accentuated our Years from Hell. Adding hefty sales increases to the travails of Phase III is something akin to throwing gasoline on a campfire. We came dangerously close to selling ourselves out of existence.

**Lesson #6**: Hiring the right consultant is not always enough. Send him where he is needed the most.

**Lesson #7**: Consultants, as proved by my two hires, come wrapped in many different packages. What you see is not always what you get. And what you get is not always what you need.

## THE BOTTOM LINE

Consultants can be powerful tools or dangerous weapons.

Network to find them, hire them with care, fire them when called for, and use them where they're needed the most.

# 19

## SPOUSES

FROM TIME TO time it is possible for entrepreneurs to have meaningful relationships with persons not directly connected with the business. When this occurs, the person being meaningfully related to (most frequently a spouse) falls into one of two categories: Blissfully Unaware or Painfully Aware.

Consider the following two scenarios:

Scenario One opens as our weary entrepreneur limps home from another day at "that place." Late for dinner as usual, entrepreneur greets Blissfully Unaware with limp handshake and glazed glance. Entrepreneur pecks spouse on cheek on way to liquor cabinet.

"The bank yanked my line today," frazzled entrepreneur blurts.

"Well, yank theirs right back," sympathizes Blissfully Unaware. "And you think you have problems? Your mother called in the middle of 'All My Children.'" (Or, depending on the gender, "And you think you have problems? The Twins traded Viola for a left-handed bullpen catcher.")

Scenario Two: Substitute Painfully Aware for Blissfully Unaware. Same background.

"The bank yanked my line today."

"Sell the lousy joint."

Painfully Aware (regardless of gender) knows that the entrepreneur lives from financial statement to financial statement and from bank committee meeting to bank committee meeting. Painfully Aware has learned that nothing will change as long as "that place" remains in the suffering entrepreneur's hands. Nothing, that is, except the size of the stakes and the amount of the analysts' fees, both of which grow in proportion to the time invested in the business.

I am married to a Painfully Aware. Like most Painfully Awares, she is a recovering Blissfully Unaware. The fact that she spent the past fifteen years in the office adjoining mine necessitated that she be as painfully aware as I.

It was often comforting that she understood. But given the choice, I would have spared her the suffering and the pain (and the helplessness) that are a part of the downsides of my chosen career.

One insomniac in the house is enough.

### THE BOTTOM LINE

Spouses have their own problems, most of which they are in a position to resolve. They are, however, rarely in a position to meaningfully affect the business.

Unless the spouse is armed with an M.B.A. or an entrepreneurial background, or unless the entrepreneur has several hours a day to review Principles of Accounting and Business 101, leave the spouse in his or her blissfully unaware state.

And God help the relationship when the spouse doesn't support the entrepreneurial commitment. A Chapter 11 or a divorce is on the horizon. Or both.

# V

## THE KEYS
## TO SUCCESS

# 20

## TEAM BUILDING AND
## COLLECTING SUPERSTARS

SHOW ME A $5-million-a-year entrepreneurial business and I'll show you a perspiring entrepreneur with a vision in his eyes.

Show me a $25-million-a-year successful and mature company and I'll show you a perspiring entrepreneur and a team of a half dozen or more productive and caring superstars with his vision in their eyes.

It follows then, that the entrepreneur's number one job, if his goal is to turn his struggling entrepreneurial business into a healthy, growing, and mature company, is to **collect a team of superstars with the entrepreneur's vision in their eyes.**

Once we've hired those superstars, we can delegate whatever our number two job might be.

Not so, however, with the process of assembling the team. It is our primary responsibility and can never be delegated. It is absolutely, assuredly the most important of all our entrepreneurial responsibilities. Nothing is even close to second!

This process of building a team of superstars consists of:

1. Locating and hiring the superstars (see chapter 32).
2. Motivating them, providing a fertile environment for

them to prosper, and compensating them (see chapters 23, 25, and 28).
3. Continual upgrading of the team at a rate as fast as or faster than the growth of the company (see chapter 29).
4. Replacing a failing superstar, when he is weakening the team (see chapter 33).

In addition to the lessons of the above-referenced chapters, here are several tips on how to build that team of superstars:

**1.** The best indicator of how any employee, superstar or otherwise, will perform in the future is how he's performed in the past. Trust yesterday's actions and not today's words when interviewing outside candidates or promoting from within.

**2.** Of all the attributes to look for in assembling your team of superstars, responsiveness to change is the most important. Resistance to change by a key member of the management team is the surest way to impede future growth and destroy opportunity.

**3.** There must be a degree of compatibility among the team members. They must agree on the company's destination and goals, and must individually subscribe to the value of a cohesive team. They need not, however, agree on the best course to pursue in reaching the destination.

**4.** When hiring superstars remember you are not hiring individual performers, you are hiring team players—individuals with a proven ability to perform in a team environment. Superstars must be able to work in a crowd and leverage themselves, for that is the key to personal business growth.

**5.** A company enjoying slow growth can, given the wide window of time it is allowed, usually find and develop superstars from within. Rapid growth almost always requires hiring from the outside, something most entrepreneurs are reluctant to do in the face of loyalty to longtime employees.

**6.** Treat superstars (and all employees, for that matter) like customers. Do whatever you can to solve their problems, then sit back and watch the good times roll.

And don't spend one-tenth of a second telling me that the reason your team of superstars isn't performing is the poor quality of its members. That's a cop-out. There are plenty of good people out there, and it's your job to find them. And hire them. And keep them.

Make no mistake about it, the problem when the team isn't performing is the entrepreneur. We've either hired the wrong superstars or we're leading the right ones in the wrong direction.

## THE BOTTOM LINE

The entrepreneur's number one job is to assure that the company is headed by a team of compatible superstars in the top five or six key management positions. This responsibility cannot be delegated.

Over prolonged periods of time, the best team always wins.

# 21

## CUSTOMER REVERENCE

REVERE THE CUSTOMER. The customer defines the business.

Listen to the customer and all good things are sure to follow.

On and on it goes. All of the above are certainly true, but why is it we have to be told? Like coming in out of the rain, customer reverence should be a conditioned response. A basic instinct.

Sadly, it isn't.

It isn't as if this concept of customer reverence is new. My mother's grocer and friend, Mr. Matulef, practiced customer reverence fifty years ago, when Tom Peters and Lee Iacocca were worrying about high school proms, not shareholders' meetings.

The difficulty in transferring this concept of customer reverence to our corporate culture comes not as a result of our inability to accept the idea, but rather from the confusing and ill-defined task of translating its premise into some form of meaningful activity. After all, 90 percent of our employees never meet a customer, yet everything we do is supposed to be conducted through the eyes of one.

The answer is that it is our job to provide a means whereby our employees learn to view the business this way. This can best be accomplished by the efficient use of the sales and customer service departments.

Sales and customer service deal with the customer every day of the week. Short of having the customer himself in front of us, sales and customer service employees are the next best thing. When they define the product, it is the customer doing the speaking. When they outline the service, it is the customer doing the outlining. They must have a voice (not the final decision, but a strong voice) in everything we do that affects the customer, from pricing and design decisions to shipping and return policies.

A warning here. It isn't without risk that we give the sales and customer service folks the degree of latitude necessary to speak for our customer. Even the best salespeople, hefty egos and all, have been known to take miles when only inches are offered. Unless we are up to the task of educating and training our sales employees on the issue of cultural balance, a generous serving of "us versus them" will become an everyday occurrence, and conflict will fill our entrepreneurial plate.

Keeping the culture balanced when so much latitude is given to so few is a situation we will have to face head on. And resolve. It takes planning and employee training from us, humility and restraint from our sales and customer service people, and understanding and patience from all of our employees to pull it off.

The development of this focus on customer needs, for those who don't have it, will require a basic change in corporate culture. "How will this decision affect our customer?" we must ask, before any discussion of change begins, rather than "How will this decision affect us?" Once the question is resolved, we are free to move on. Not before.

OK, enough, you say. Enough of this theory. How do we apply the love-of-the-customer premise to our small company? Where do we start tomorrow morning?

**1. You've gotta see one to know one.** Put your key employees, including all of your superstars, in front of a customer on a semiregular basis. Your execs, along with selected design and manufacturing folks, should get off their duffs and out of their offices, and tag along on a sales call at least once a month. Salespeople will initially balk at this arrangement since they don't like anybody (especially management) peering over their shoulders while they work.

It is the entrepreneur's responsibility, however, to educate sales to accept this gotta-see-one-to-know-one sales call as another way to make their job easier and serve their customers better. Sales must learn that the process of introducing key players to the customer can only help everybody win.

**2. Streamline the customer service department.** Make it user friendly. Give customer service an additional, direct (unlisted) hot line and hand out that number to only the most deserving customers. This will not only shorten key customer response time, it will also boost customer service's ego.

**3. Reverse the new product process.** The old product development process goes something like this: 1) produce the product, and 2) find the customer.

Reverse the process. Begin with a customer, discover a need, and fill that need with a product. Educate the sales department and then demand that it ask and listen (if it doesn't already) for customer needs. Explore fresh niches and search for new products, rather than reshape old ones.

**4. Hire the fire in their eyes.** Build a sales force where the big guys don't. Let them raid the established pipeline and pay the old-timers big bucks to sell the same tired products as before. Meanwhile, hire sales employees for character, not for experience. To sell solutions, not commodities. Today's salespeople require a much different set of skills than yesterday's, with listening at the top of the list. Today's sales are made with the ears, not the mouth.

And don't be confined by the spirit of tradition in the sales hiring process. Someone unique, which salespeople must be, is rarely found among today's crusty veterans.

The two best salespeople I ever hired walked in off the street. One strolled in unannounced, the other in response to a help-wanted ad. Their résumés were blank. Their eyes were not. I hired the fire in their eyes.

**5. Rules are made to be bent.** I'll bend just about anything in order to keep an old customer or ink a new one. (It costs six times as much to find new customers as it does to keep old ones.) Rigid rules may work for the marine corps and the IRS, but what do those folks know about putting a smile on the face of a customer?

The late Sam Walton took this premise one step further. His favorite rule? "Break all rules."

**6. Establish a customer feedback system.** Give the sales department input on everything, from product design to the way the telephone is answered. Set up a customer feedback system allowing the sales department a channel by which to give instant feedback on the latest reactions from their customers.

An effective option for customer feedback is the annual report card, a once-a-year survey of the best customers asking them to respond to a limited number of key questions. The questions should be designed to measure the company's progress in solving problems as well as to emit danger signals.

**7. Change the format of sales meetings.** Ask the heads of every other department to attend a designated segment of every sales meeting. Instead of focusing on sales opportunities, use that portion of the meeting to share customer feedback.

**8. Sell quality and service, not price.** Zombies sell price. Why waste a good sales force? Selling for price won't build relationships with anybody, except maybe the work-out department at the bank.

**9. Make manufacturing a marketing tool.** Train the manufacturing department on the importance of responding to customer needs, and encourage them to take customer ideas, funneled through the sales department, and turn them into new products. Given the opportunity, most manufacturing employees will jump at the chance to become a part of the sales process. Then sit back and watch the orders roll in.

**10. Teach Accounting 101.** Train the salespeople to read profit and loss statements and understand the rudiments of profitability. Their tendency to move and to shake will filter all the way down to the bottom line, if they are given a background and a reason to care.

**11. Pay commission based on profitability, not on volume.** Like number 10 above, this may not contribute directly to customer reverence, but it sure will do wonders for the bottom line.

It's an immutable rule of the universe that when salespeople change employers, they take the majority of their best customers with them. As much as we would prefer it otherwise, the relationship is not between our customer and us, it is between our customer and the salesperson (a lesson I've learned the hard way more than once). The moral? Learn to trust our salespeople to speak for our customers, because no one else has the opportunity to understand them.

Customer reverence is the only answer if we are to survive in a marketplace where everybody, including our competitors, has caught on to it. Today's winners (and tomorrow's survivors) will be those who are successful at translating the theory of customer reverence into a companywide mentality.

We alone set the culture of our company. Nobody else. If we want our company to become focused on the customer through our sales and service departments, then by God, it will. If we don't, it won't.

We must learn for ourselves, and subsequently educate our employees, that there is only one desired result of our company's combined efforts: the customer making a conscious decision to exchange his cash for our product.

All other things we do are only events leading up to that result.

Our focus should be on results, not events.

## THE BOTTOM LINE

The secret to keeping a customer? Undercommit and over-deliver.

The sales and customer service departments are the mouth of the customer. The entrepreneur's job is to provide them with a forum from which to speak. And an audience that is willing to listen.

It is only cultural change that can develop customer reverence, and the ability to cause cultural change lies entirely in the entrepreneur's hands.

If you don't learn to revere your customer, someone else will.

# 22

## A COMMITMENT
## TO QUALITY

I LOST $18 million one day in 1972.

That day was National Screenprint's first day of business. I was there as the first shirt rolled down our dryer belt. I didn't know it at the time, but during the course of that day the workmanship of one out of every twenty shirts we would print would be something less than our customer would consider acceptable. I can say this now with some degree of certainty after eighteen years in the business.

I set the quality standards for our company that day. Not by what I did but by what I didn't do. I didn't reject a single shirt. Not one. I let mediocrity stream down the belt and roll unmolested into the packing boxes. I didn't take a stand on behalf of perfection. I made no clamor for quality. Our customers and our employees would know our product forever by my actions that day, and we would live with the consequences for eighteen long and expensive years.

Perhaps I wanted to save the two bucks that each mediocre shirt represented. Or maybe I didn't want to hurt a printer's feelings, or spoil the euphoria of opening day.

How was I to know (I rationalize now) that hundreds of thousands of National Screenprint products over the years would be produced and go unrejected, thanks to the example I set that day? How was I to know that my acceptance of mediocrity would cost us countless hours of rework time, and invoicing credits, and spoilage write-offs, and (the most telling hit) an untold number of customers who would take their business elsewhere?

Whatever my motives, mediocrity became acceptable at National Screenprint on our opening day of business in 1972.

The cost? In 1988 we attempted to put a pencil to nonquality, as best we could. The exercise was not exactly steeped in science, given the many gray areas involved. More than a few assumptions had to be made. But the results were believable. And frightening.

We determined that acceptance of mediocrity cost us 12 percent of every sales dollar! Meaning that my stance that first day cost National Screenprint $18 million over the nineteen years of our existence. Not to mention millions of dollars in sales volume and profits lost as a result of departed customers.

We initiated a companywide quality program in 1988—it's never too late. A year and a half later I was still struggling to get the program and the new culture off the ground when National Screenprint was sold. In the meantime my commitment to the quality program and our success with it had been short-circuited by the Years from Hell.

If it is true that we learn more from our mistakes than we do from our successes, then I qualify as one of industry's foremost experts on the subject of quality. Here is a taste of the lessons I learned:

**1.** The position of quality in the company culture is established on that first day. Once the culture is in place, it is easier to get rid of Saddam Hussein than it is to effect a companywide change.

**2.** The entrepreneur's commitment to a quality program must be chiseled in stone. Unalterable. Words alone won't work, and as a matter of fact will have the opposite effect if not followed up by action. It is better not to start a quality program at all if the entrepreneur's commitment isn't behind it.

False starts or promises will only destroy credibility and make it impossible to build a quality-oriented culture.

**3.** There are many quality programs to choose from. Buy one or create one. Some probably work better than others, but if the commitment is there, most programs will succeed.

**4.** Some of the quality program chores can be delegated by the entrepreneur, but the commitment to the program and responsibility for its success cannot.

**5.** Moments of truth can kill a quality program. The moments when the entrepreneur stands face-to-face with those expensive, monumental, culture-altering decisions. You'll know when one of those moments arrives, and it always results in a severe, painful, bottom-line hit. Overcoming those moments of truth is, however, a necessary part of the process of overriding the past. If they go undisturbed and unresolved, or are resolved in a look-the-other-way manner, the quality program is as good as dead.

**6.** Quality must be number one on the entrepreneur's mind for the first two or three years of the program. If cash flow or sales or even survival takes over, the quality program is doomed to defeat—or to mediocrity, the reason the issue of quality arose in the first place.

The best time to start a quality program is when things are going smoothly and you can devote your full attention to it. And don't stoke up a quality program in the midst of an already chaotic Phase III.

**7.** Associated costs are staggering during the first year of a quality program. A host of unfamiliar expense categories show up on the P&L, in addition to the hidden costs that are always buried in loss of margin. Those new hits hurt, especially when earnings are already slim or nonexistent.

**8.** There are thousands of companies in the United States today with successful quality programs in place. Most are justifiably proud of what they have accomplished and will share the story of their success. There are national quality councils, books, videos, and quality newsletters. There are consultants and quality companies waiting in the wings for opportunities exactly like yours. Lack of available information is not an excuse for postponing the kickoff of a quality program.

**9.** The time it takes to resolve a past infested with mediocrity is expressed not in months, but in years. Or in decades, depending on your goals. Or never, some say. But improvements can start tomorrow, and there will be benefits every day.

Quality, or the lack thereof, is not confined to the product or service we offer. It can show up everywhere.

In the early 1970s Adidas had a lock on the athletic footwear market. Like Drexel and Salomon of recent times, Adidas flaunted its success in the face of the very customers who put it on top. The company welcomed new customers when it was unable to satisfy old ones, and made delivery commitments it was unable to keep. On-time delivery went the way of the wooden tennis racket. The shipping department shipped whatever it wished, whenever it wished. Manufacturing workmanship declined, invoices were incorrect, and new company policies infuriated old-line customers on a daily basis. Customers needed the product but hated the company.

This across-the-board display of nonquality caused Adidas to pay the price. Reebok and Nike saw to that.

The failure to address and overcome quality shortcomings is not an abstract issue with most of us entrepreneurs. Our problem in making a successful commitment to a quality program is that several typical traits stand in our way. Included among them are:

**1. Aversion to conflict.** Cultural changes involving such deeply inbred traits as quality awareness never occur without a substantial amount of conflict, particularly in the early stages of a quality program, as old habits must be challenged and changed. There will be a number of old-line employees who will fight the changes to the bitter end.

**2. Attention to detail.** A successful quality program requires unflagging attention to detail on the part of the entrepreneur for extended periods of time.

**3. Prolonged focus.** The pursuit of a quality program requires unerring focus on a goal, often to the exclusion of other projects that are more to an entrepreneur's liking. And, since mediocrity is currently the norm and will not be altered easily, this shift in focus needs to be maintained for long periods of time.

**4. Tedious work.** The establishment and maintenance of quality programs is not something that most entrepreneurs consider exciting—the action is slow and tedious, and short-term results are often difficult to measure. The road to quality can be, well, downright boring, especially to those of us who get our kicks from sales and marketing.

Quality, or the lack thereof, begins with the entrepreneur. We can delegate the tasks of the quality program but never the commitment. We can assign the performance to others but not the responsibility. And we can pass on the accolades but not the accountability.

It is a testimony to the times that every company, entrepreneurial or otherwise, must make a commitment to improve their quality. Mediocrity as an acceptable business culture is on its way out.

Our company will be, too, if we don't get on board.

### THE BOTTOM LINE

Quality is defined on the opening day of business by the actions of the entrepreneur. Your personal quality standards, or lack thereof, ultimately become the standards of your company. A light-hearted commitment to quality is worse than no commitment at all.

Attainment of acceptable quality, in itself, will not ensure the survival of your business. But a lack of acceptable quality will ensure its failure.

Customer expectations should be the yardstick for measuring quality.

Quality lost takes years to regain.

# 23

# EMPLOYEE OWNERSHIP

EMPLOYEES WHO ARE minority shareholders can be a pain in the neck. Which is not to say I didn't have any. Or wouldn't again.

What the heck, if I were a minority shareholder in a privately held business, I'd probably be a pain in the neck, too. Capitalism, the feds, the state we live in, and the unethical history of some of our entrepreneurial predecessors have rightfully awarded the minority shareholder his license to annoy.

Minority shareholders come in two categories, those that are necessary and helpful to the future of the business, and those that are not. Necessary and helpful minority shareholders include those folks who are valuable employees and those whose investment is currently needed to keep the balance sheet banker friendly.

Those who aren't necessary include all ex-employees, relatives, friends, investors whose cash is no longer needed, and just about everybody else who comes to mind. When in doubt, the rule goes, cash them out.

Then use that opportunity to get those cashed-in stock certificates into a good employee's hands. The more the merrier, if we've collected and trained the kind of employees we want as partners. Sure, even our best employees can, and will, turn into a pain in the neck, but on balance the trade-off is worth the trouble.

There isn't a contemporary business book written that doesn't extol the obvious virtues of employee ownership as a motivating tool. The increased commitment that comes from ownership is well worth the associated headaches that are bound to evolve. This fact is well documented, it's tangible, it makes sense, and anybody who has grown a successful company with key employees in the role of part owners can attest to the benefits.

Several thoughts that come from experience on the subject of minority employee ownership:

**1.** Establish strategic objectives before making share number one available to anybody, employee or otherwise. Spell out guidelines and policies and logical reasons to determine who should have the opportunity to buy company stock and, just as important, who will not. Once the word is out that stock is available, requests to buy will come from every imaginable nook and cranny. You must be able to explain the logic and consistency behind your determination of who may purchase shares and, at the same time, avoid offending those excluded.

**2.** Involve a lawyer in every stock deal, no matter how insignificant it seems. I know, this means more legal fees, but you need the protection of the buy-sell agreements and purchase agreements and disclaimers and all those downside-avoidance documents that lawyers specialize in and entrepreneurs don't. And whatever your lawyer plugs in, you can count on the fact that it still won't be enough if irate employees/shareholders leave the company and determine that you have violated their inalienable shareholder rights.

**3.** If you aren't prepared (or can't muster the patience) to answer the tough questions that are bound to come, then don't even consider taking on minority shareholders, employees or otherwise. They have a legal right to ask questions, and the knowledgeable ones will (wouldn't you?). If you take offense at their interrogation, no matter how pointed, the benefits of having employees as shareholders will soon be offset by the drawbacks. (This is an ego issue you're facing here, nothing more.)

**4.** Once you are committed to employee ownership, by far the best route to go is an ESOP. There are standard ESOPs whereby company earnings are contributed to an ESOP trust in the name of employees. There are leveraged ESOPs in which a bank loans money to the employees (behind the entrepreneur's guarantee) to buy the stock. Even the federal government loves ESOPs, and allows the IRS to grant a slew of generous tax advantages to their participants.

Your company must be extremely healthy to make a leveraged ESOP work, however—the balance sheet strong, earnings steady, and the outlook rosy. This is particularly true in today's restrictive financial climate where banks go out of their way to find reasons not to do deals.

**5.** A handshake and a smile when handing out stock certificates do not complete the entrepreneur's list of new-found shareholder responsibilities once the decision has been made to share ownership. Be prepared to provide a whole new genre of corporate communications on both a regularly scheduled and an as-needed basis. These include shareholder meetings, earnings reports, changes in shareholders, and notification of important developments affecting the value of the stock.

The decision whether or not to offer stock in the company to the people who are responsible for building it is, in truth, a no-brainer. But we must consider our ability to perform our new shareholder-in-chief duties and to adjust to the specter of letting the shareholders annoy us before committing ourselves to anything so rash.

If our ego gives us the green light, there is no valid reason to say no.

## THE BOTTOM LINE

Employee ownership is on the rise and for good reason. It works.

The introduction of minority shareholders does not necessarily make the entrepreneur's life any easier. Autocratic entrepreneurs should either look for other ways to motivate employees, or overcome their dictatorial ways. I suggest the latter.

Dictatorial entrepreneurs and minority shareholders are destined to clash. Nobody wins when they do.

# 24

## THE RIGHT

## NICHE

IACOCCA ON THE payroll and the Bible disguised as a business plan won't make a smidgen of difference to our success if our product is scuba gear and the market is Greenland. There are no Northwest Trading outlets in Mozambique. No Panama Jacks in Antarctica.

The niche comes first.

Niches come in many shapes and forms. Some are low-tech and wide, some high-tech and narrow, and some at points between. They provide opportunities for the courageous, quicksand for the foolish, and guarantees to none.

Looking for a major-league return on your investment? Danger and intrigue? Indigestion, stress, and trauma? The high-tech and narrow niche may be for you.

Bill Gates and Steve Jobs are high-tech and narrow-niche guys. As well as thousands of others currently not answering phone calls.

Those high-tech windows spring open suddenly, almost without warning, as a new technology appears. The rush is on for a short time before the window slams shut as quickly as it opened.

The fleet of foot make it inside, but the majority don't get their feet off the ground. A few are caught straddling the sill when the window crashes.

Those high-tech niches with their crashing windows and winner-take-all poker games are not for everyone. The world of small business abounds with the low-tech and wide-niche players, where windows are forever, and technological changes occur over years, not days. Where the difference is in the way we smile at our customers, keep our overhead down, and make our plans while competitors sleep.

The successful niche picker will find a niche that others ignore. He knows that the more visible and more appealing the niche, the more crowded it becomes. Many of us have dreamed about the sporting goods industry since Little League days, but so has everybody else. As a result that niche is overflowing with legions of sweating pantsers and entrepreneurs, and its gross margins react accordingly. The effects of supply and demand are never far away.

The niche must also suit the temperament of the entrepreneur. Many of us don't have the will or the stomach to compete against the odds that Gates and Jobs face, no matter what the potential return.

Personally, I have no desire to live eternally on the edge. I don't need an endless stack of cash to keep me happy. Many of us can be comfortable in our low-tech and wide niches, where it's the little things that make the difference, and life doesn't hinge on yesterday's lost gamble or tomorrow's new gizmo.

Gates and Jobs would grow white beards in my niches. I'd have triple bypasses in theirs.

### THE BOTTOM LINE

The niche should attract the entrepreneur and not vice versa.

Pick a niche where everybody isn't, and one that suits

your interests, your skills, and your comfort zone. The niche you discover may beckon seductively, but if it is crowded or the chemistry isn't right, leave that opportunity for others.

There is no end to the availability of viable niches for those willing to be patient.

# 25

# A BALANCED

# CULTURE

NATIONAL SCREENPRINT HAD five geographically dispersed production centers in 1989, each fully armed with sales, production, accounting, administrative, and art departments. Five location managers ruled their entrepreneurial fiefdoms with five distinct management styles. Each manager established and maintained his or her own corporate culture, consistent with their talents and beliefs.

Two of the five managers came from operational backgrounds. Not surprisingly, their locations developed strong production cultures. Meanwhile, their salespeople were not treated like Lindbergh when he landed in Paris. There was a constant diet of production-versus-sales problems on the agenda of these two managers.

A third manager came from a strong sales background. Too few sales were never a problem here. Too many sales were, and the necessary support services were rarely in place to handle this production center's relentless sales increases. Disgruntled salespeople and their equally disgruntled customers combined to keep this manager dashing from crisis to crisis.

Sales employees barked directions to the support employees.

Not surprisingly, the revolving door for support employees spun ceaselessly. Production spoilage was twice the company average, quality a misnomer, production efficiency an oxymoron.

The remaining two locations were managed with no discernible managerial tilt in either direction. These two managers, strong administrators both, maintained a healthy balance between sales and production, throwing in a sufficient portion of accounting and administration for good measure. Heroes came from everywhere.

Quiz time now. Notebooks inside your desks. Pencils ready:

Answer the following questions with an A, B, or C. (A for production-oriented culture, B for sales-oriented culture, or C for balanced culture.)

1. Which of the five locations were always the most profitable?
2. Which of the five locations managed their assets the best?
3. Which of the five locations required the least corporate assistance?
4. Which of the five managers received the largest bonuses?
5. Which of the five managers complained least about the compensation system?

Time's up.

If you answered C to all the above, you get an A. Let's face it, compensation plans usually favor the sales employees. And rightfully so in a system where nothing happens until a sale is made, with moderation being the key. Unfortunately, however, these often open-ended compensation plans can carry an unbalanced message to the remainder of the employees.

If we are biased toward sales ourselves, whether as the result of background, education, or personal belief, a cultural imbalance is bound to evolve within the company. We must recognize the existence of this imbalance, and, acting in our role as cultural leader, take steps to correct it.

In the likely event that we are unable to assure the desired balance by changing our own bias, we need to hire a counter-weight, someone to offset it. Given our typical sales orientation, that counterweight should either be a president with strong administrative and financial skills or a first-rate, strongly supported CFO. And we must delegate to the counterweight the degree of authority necessary to effect those cultural changes.

While never enraptured with compensation packages that favor sales, most employees will learn to accept unbalanced paychecks. But they will never learn to accept a lopsided culture.

A sampling of important cultural tips I've collected over the years:

**1.** What you say has nothing to do with establishing your company's culture. It is only what you do that matters.

**2.** Cultures start developing on the entrepreneur's first day on the job, as the employees observe their boss's every move. Be aware of their ongoing and relentless scrutiny and assure that the messages you send are designed to encourage the culture you publicly espouse.

**3.** Most successful growth companies feature cultures that encourage risk taking and allow first-time mistakes. As with skiing and gymnastics, you can't learn and improve in an environment where you aren't allowed to fall down.

**4.** Change is inevitable, and corporate culture needs changing from time to time. Take steps to inventory and alter your existing culture when it no longer represents what is best for your company.

**5.** The acquisitional entrepreneur should not underestimate the difficulty in changing the culture of an acquired company. The road to change will take twice as long as planned, and casualties will be twice as heavy. Go slow.

The same is true when cultures need changing within your existing company. Change never occurs as quickly as the entrepreneur would like.

We should take a physical inventory of our corporate culture every year or two. This can be done by polling the employees on such cultural categories as honesty, open communications, recognition, teamwork, balance, expense awareness, commitment to quality, concern for employees, and customer reverence. Subsequent examination of our culture may call for the insertion of a missing piece, or the revision of an existing one.

## THE BOTTOM LINE

Corporate culture is a company's value system. It flows from only one source—the top.

Cultural change is not a process, but an evolution. Time is its friend, impatience its enemy.

A corporate culture cannot change unless the entrepreneur changes. Or unless he delegates the authority to change and then stands aside.

Culture responds to the entrepreneur's actions, not to his words.

# 26

## CLARITY

NATIONAL SCREENPRINT STUMBLED into our Years from Hell with significant inventory and accounts receivable problems: low inventory turns, high inventory shrinkage, inadequate accounting systems, large LIFO write-downs, archaic credit policies, and on and on into the depressing world of shrinking assets.

As our asset management problems worsened, I made my CFO's life miserable. Not surprisingly, this didn't help. Finally, I could stand it no more. How, I asked him, in the name of marginal bean counting, could he continue to hold his head high in the face of such dismal results?

"Excuse me, Jim," said he without batting an eyelash, "but I wasn't aware that asset management was my responsibility."

"But," I sputtered, "everybody knows that the CFO manages corporate assets. I mean—I can't believe—surely you're jesting?"

He wasn't.

Here I was paying $55,000 a year to a guy who wasn't even sure what his job entailed.

But should he have to ask?

At about the same time, I hired a consultant to train me and our managers on a variety of subjects tied to individual job performance, corporate planning, and strategy. During one heated session, with all eight of our key managers in attendance, the consultant inquired of each of us, "What are National Screenprint's mission and goals, and why are you here?"

"I'm paying good money for this?" I can remember thinking at the time.

Eight random answers later, the now smug consultant had made his painful point. Each of our managers had a different idea of why we existed, where we were going, how we were going to get there, and what his or her role was in our journey. If the understanding of our eight top managers was this vague, I realized, what in hell must our remaining 192 employees be thinking?

My entrepreneurial, small-potato mentality needed to be overcome. No longer was I capable of performing every job in the company. No longer was I the right person to make all the important decisions. No longer was my perception of where the company was headed sufficient to get us there.

All employees, I learned, needed a foundation for the decisions required in their jobs. An understanding of our mission, a familiarity with our goals, an overview of our reason for existence.

The word *clarity* began to evolve in our corporate culture about that time. Our monthly newsletter featured articles and columns on such fuzzy and misunderstood subjects as culture, mission, goals, and strategy as applied to our company. We instituted regularly scheduled employee meetings, with the primary purpose of presenting and discussing issues related to overview and understanding, rather than specifics and operations.

We developed job descriptions for every position in the company, to avoid further definitional problems like the one I had with the CFO. I had always cringed at the thought of formal job descriptions, considering them to be limiting, all the while encouraging employees to work in a vacuum. But job descriptions can be written loosely or tightly, restrictively or openly, and can be engineered to do whatever the entrepreneur intends. And besides providing a definition of employees' responsibilities, job descriptions give us a basis on which to measure their performance.

We demanded clarification on day-to-day communication issues. We encouraged our employees to be sure they knew the answers to the following questions: Exactly what is wanted here? Why is this necessary? What results are expected? By when? How will my performance be measured?

There would be no more National Screenprint employees, I promised myself, CFO or otherwise, who would fail because of misunderstanding. Failure would henceforth be caused by an employee's commission, not by my omission.

Clarity does not always come naturally to entrepreneurs. Like culture, it takes time to develop and is a child of patience.

Good managers have patience. Most entrepreneurs don't.

## THE BOTTOM LINE

Clarity must take over from vague expectations when your company grows to the point where you are no longer capable of being everywhere at once.

If you aren't clear in defining where it is you are going, how can you expect your employees to get there?

And if you have never explained where "there" is, how will they know when they've arrived?

# 27

## ACCOUNTABILITY

I LEARNED EARLY on in life how accountability can work to a person's advantage. I was still in grade school, maybe fourth grade or so, when Punch Brown (short for One Punch Brown, because that's all it usually took) decided he needed my protractor to consummate some sinister deed.

"Give it back or else," I quaked to Punch.

"Or else what?" he growled.

"Or else—I'll tell Miss Brody." It was a stab in the dark.

It worked! He flashed me a hand signal popular at the time, returned my protractor, and lumbered off to harass some other skinny kid.

Looking back, I know now why it worked. Nobody messed with Miss Brody, not even Punch Brown. If she told you not to do something and you did it anyway, you were history. Yesterday's news. We all knew what Miss Brody expected from us, and she clearly communicated our punishment if we chose not to perform. When we did act against her wishes, she would follow up. In spades. You could set your Dick Tracy wristwatch by it.

What a great manager Miss Brody would have been. She had

Punch Brown, no prize kid, firmly in the palm of her hand. If she could handle Punch, I know now, she could handle anybody.

Miss Brody had learned somewhere along the line that there are two elements to the process of establishing accountability: communication of expectations and follow-up.

As a journeyman manager, I showed mild improvement in making people accountable once I understood the role of clarity in the management equation. Any doubt in my mind of the necessity of clearly laying out my expectations was dispelled by the case of the shrinking corporate assets.

My biggest problem was always with follow-up. Not the kind of follow-up necessary after a job was done well, because that was always fun. Most of us enjoy leaving a trail of smiles in our wake, and I was no exception. My problem was with the kind of follow-up required when performance did not measure up to expectation. You know, the follow-up that inevitably ends in confrontation. And conflict.

I would accept the flimsiest excuses known to man in my relentless determination to avoid conflict. Of course I understood why poor old Joe was too busy to get the job done. And naturally I sympathized with Helen, because the art department would never cooperate with me, either. We'll get them the next time, I would sagely counsel, and send the failed, but relieved, manager off with a pat on the back and a tousle of the hair.

Anything to get us both off the hook.

Consequently, performance to goals and objectives was not a priority around National Screenprint. Multiplying our problems, I surrounded myself with managers of similar soft and forgiving characteristics. Nice folks all, but few of them felt any pressing need to perform to anybody's expectations, least of all mine.

Those who build businesses from nothing are prone to assume that employees' motives for performing their assigned tasks are similar to ours. We perform because we have this internal mechanism inside us, driving us to create something, to improve something, to make something better.

Average employees are not so motivated. (Which doesn't make them wrong, only different.) Most are looking for something else—security, perhaps, or income, or recognition. Maybe a combination of the three. It is up to us to either recognize these differences and manage around them, or give our employees the opportunity, and the latitude, to alter their motivation to something similar to ours.

This need to communicate expectations and then follow up, both positively and negatively, should be nothing new to many of us.

Those of us who are parents have been doing it for years.

## THE BOTTOM LINE

Conflict is natural to the process of achieving accountability. One does not come without the other.

Accountability for performance requires clear expectations and both positive and negative follow-up.

Nice guys finish last when consequences for nonperformance are not an element of the accountability equation.

# 28

## COMPENSATION

PEOPLE WHO STUDY such things tell us that the average employee considers compensation to be number five on his or her list of motivators (behind appreciation, information, understanding, and job security). This news is encouraging to our nation's economic future, I say, but irrelevant when salary review time comes around. Mother Teresa turns into Muhammad Ali when wages are on the line.

Then, compensation is the employees' foremost motivator, and conflict is at the top of their minds. The degree of conflict experienced will depend upon the breadth of their expectations, the extent of the entrepreneur's largesse, and the kind of employees they happen to be.

Where compensation is concerned, employees fall into four categories: revolvers, dependables, movers and shakers, and executives.

Revolvers are entry-level employees in for the short haul. Their primary motivation is to accumulate enough cash to get them through the weekend; they don't intend to be around six months from now. (The more low-tech and labor-intensive the company, the more revolvers we will see come and go.)

Revolvers hire on at the advertised wage. Working just long enough to accept their ninety-day bump, they mosey on down the road when the winds change, which generally coincides with the times they are needed the most. Compensation reviews are minor inconveniences to them, since their employment usually doesn't last long enough for pay increases to become an issue.

Dependables are those employees in for the long haul. They are most likely to come to the compensation table armed to the teeth, because they view themselves not as dependables but as indispensables. (Valuable they are, indispensable they are not.)

They have studied all the applicable state and federal laws and know their rights thereunder. They are ready, willing, and able to compare and discuss wages with any of their fellow employees who will lend them an ear.

Extreme care must be exercised throughout the compensation process when dealing with dependables. The entrepreneur must be consistent and fair to the nth degree, and always cover his tracks. Nickels and dimes are important to dependables, and details can be deal breakers. One unhappy dependable can cause more damage to company morale than an overlooked Christmas bonus check.

Compensation rationale for dependables should be consistent, definitive, and defined for all to see. Since most of them know how much their peers are making, it is important there be a distinct methodology to the compensation schedule. Small disparities will beget big problems.

Meanwhile, the movers and shakers (our product champions and sales folks) belly up to the compensation table with their motives exposed. We know exactly where they stand and what turns them on. With some it's money, or the opportunity to make a ton of it. With others, it's the chance to make a difference and grow with the company. The financial reward, while important, is secondary. Nickels and dimes and details are not important to them. Open ends and opportunities are.

Compensation plans for our movers and shakers require creativity, adaptability, and as few topside limits (within reason) as possible. These plans should include commission (based on profitability) for the salespeople, and a base salary with well-defined bonuses based on the performance of their product for the product-development folks.

Finally we have the executives. When determining executive pay, individual creativity is allowable, but the performance of the team must be a part of the package and should always override individual performances. The true team players will understand this. I recommend (in the absence of companywide pay-for-performance plans) a modest base salary featuring annual cost-of-living increases and the opportunity to earn sizable bonuses (paid quarterly if cash flow will allow it), to be based on a combination of personal and team achievements. Bonuses should always be paid for performance as opposed to by an agreed-upon plan.

A CFO friend of mine tells the story of a creative, homegrown management bonus program that his entrepreneurial boss assembled for him. The package included several key asset-management goals but not overall corporate profitability.

His company posted significant P&L losses for the year, even as the CFO achieved the asset-management goals assigned to him. He walked into his boss's office at the end of the year with hand outstretched, expecting his just reward.

The boss inflated, as my friend tells it, like a prairie chicken in heat. The CFO escaped with his life and job intact, and their relationship survived the incident. Barely.

Oh yes. My friend did not get his bonus.

Moral: In the interests of clarity and team building, include overall corporate profitability as a qualifier in any executive bonus packages. A side effect of this will be that the achieving managers in the organization will not be shy about *demanding* that something be done about peers who don't measure up.

The American Compensation Association tells us that pay-for-performance plans are becoming increasingly popular in the United States, from Fortune 500–size companies on down. Paying for performance is an enlightened alternative to the old-fashioned method of paying for time.

Pay-for-performance (also called gain sharing or success sharing) plans can be designed to reward employees in several ways.

Individual plans recognize individual performance (an offshoot of piecework). Work-unit plans reward teams or departments. And company plans recognize the performance of the entire company.

The "performance" that we wish to encourage when establishing pay-for-performance plans can be expressed in a variety of goals. Profitability (measured in dollars), productivity (measured in work units), quality, attendance, or a mixture of the above.

Most pay-for-performance plans are accompanied by employee-involvement programs, designed to give the employees a more active voice in making the decisions that impact their jobs. This increased involvement allows the individual employees (after all, who can do it better?) to create the working environment that best encourages productivity, or quality, or whatever the goal happens to be.

Pay for performance has several not always beneficial side effects. It is union unfriendly: most unions see management and employee collusion as a threat to their existence. It also increases the burden on the accounting department, or whoever is responsible for measurement. The necessary systems should be in place to measure performance before exciting the employees about such a plan.

It is important that all employees be included in, and treated consistently by, a pay-for-performance plan. If, for instance, executive pay goes up, then compensation of all (except commissioned) employees should follow. Everyone shares. Or everyone doesn't.

A collection of sundry tips on the general subject of compensation:

**1.** Creativity is acceptable in the compensation process, as long as the employee understands all of its components. Don't, for instance, design programs based on such formulas as return on assets unless you have thoroughly educated and trained your employees on exactly what ROA is, how it is determined, and what each person can do to positively (or negatively) affect it.

And don't even think about rewarding ROA (or any other formula) if you aren't capable of measuring it on a current and ongoing basis.

**2.** Pay is only one piece of the compensation puzzle. There are also numerous, but shrinking, perks and bennies that can be awarded in lieu of the paycheck. Stock options (an individualized form of pay for performance) are a favorite for public or privately held companies willing to share their equity.

**3.** The entrepreneur's personal compensation is always guesstimated by his employees, usually semiaccurately. Internal networks in small businesses are strong and surprisingly accurate. If he pays himself big bucks even as the company and the employees earn little, watch the tongues wag. Or worse.

**4.** Consider an ESOP. It is an effective tool by which to empower employees, hand out bonuses, retain cash in the company, and receive tax benefits, all at the same time.

**5.** Keep the periods of time between bonus payments as short as possible. A year is too long. And pay the bonuses on time; don't try to earn interest on money due to employees.

There are people for hire who study the subject of compensation and incentives. They write books and hold seminars. They consult and design custom compensation and incentive packages. Try them. Trial and error is a painful way to learn the lessons of compensation.

I always welcomed the end of salary-fixing season. That time of year was rife with conflict, especially during our Years from Hell, when the accompanying lack of profitability dictated disappointment on both sides of the table.

It's tough to divvy up what you don't have but not what you do have.

When times are good, it's time to share.

## THE BOTTOM LINE

Compensation may not be the number one employee motivator, but when a competitor comes looking to steal the best ones, compensation is usually his foot in the door.

Broaden the compensation package beyond base pay, and always consider rewarding team performance rather than the individual, except in the case of salespeople.

Compensation should be viewed as a strategy, not as a cost of doing business. Compensation plans should be designed with the intent of improving employee performance and achieving forecast goals.

# 29

---

# TRAINING

---

WE HAVE PREVIOUSLY established (chapter 20) that the number one responsibility of an entrepreneur (or manager, or president) is to surround himself with a team of superstars. It is difficult to argue with this statement. But assembling a team of superstars is only the initial stage of the team-building process. We also must keep them performing at superstar levels.

For those of us with rapidly growing companies, it is not easy for all our employees to keep pace with growth. Back-to-back years of 25-percent growth means that our team of superstars (including ourselves) must continue to increase their management skills by at least a similar percentage.

Training is the most efficient and least expensive answer to ongoing employee improvement, but unfortunately it remains close to the bottom on the entrepreneur's priority list. Like the golfer who needs to mow the lawn, we know training is important, but we always seem to have something better to do.

Training is the number one unsung and unused implement in our all-too-small bag of personal improvement tools. It is relegated to infrequent use as we follow our trusty pantser blueprints, which call for trial and error as the primary learning device.

A young friend of mine who went the pinstripe route with Xerox tells me that in his first year of employment he spent five full months in formal training. Tack on another full month of reading and study, and several more months of on-the-job training, and my friend had more training in one year than I had in twenty. By a multiple of five. Ditto for most of my employees.

I have no idea whether Xerox's approach is the right one— my friend tells me there is some overkill in those numbers. But Xerox's research must indicate, to their management at least, that those training dollars will ultimately pay dividends. Meanwhile, we of the entrepreneurial and undercapitalized world earmark our earnings for such mundane necessities as financing inventory, receivables, or operations. We need output from our employees, not diplomas. Or so we think.

Thus training rarely gets the attention that it deserves. We complain we can't take the time away from our job or there is too much to do on that particular day or that particular week. Not to mention that training on such subjects as communications, or accountability, or systems and controls has the same effect on most of us as two pounds of Thanksgiving turkey followed by a Tampa Bay football game.

Training comes in many forms and from various sources. Unlike our big-business cousins with their sophisticated in-house training departments, most of us must get our instruction from the outside, as inside pickings are usually slim. Consultants, seminars, schooling, and books are our primary options. I've tried them all.

Consultants have the most potential, but are also the most expensive and carry the heaviest risk (see chapter 18). Seminars can also be expensive in both dollars and time, while their potential value is difficult to predict in advance. The good ones are great bargains, the bad ones outlandish scams. The trick is to learn up front how to make the distinction. Schooling, while more dependable than seminars, is still difficult to predict. Teachers come in many forms.

A book is the ultimate bargain. Buy it for little or borrow it for nothing. Read it between projects, put it down when you please, and refer to it always. Keep it forever or pass it on to a friend or an employee. Extract one idea, no matter how small, and the ten or twenty bucks are quickly repaid, many times over. Every idea after the first is a bonus.

Once we've located the training that is best for us and once we've applied it where it's needed the most, our job is not finished. Our old friend follow-up must be called upon once more, or our training expenditures will yield nothing more than a quick energy infusion along with a needless expense. Successful follow-up is accomplished by assuring that all training expenditures are immediately translated into some form of positive action: the development of new systems, new programs, new ideas, or altered behaviors.

A few hard-earned tips on the subject of training:

**1.** Cross training is the one training device that can be utilized entirely with inside resources. It is inexpensive and benefits everybody.

**2.** Every company should offer a tuition-reimbursement program to its employees whereby their expenses for related outside studies are reimbursed. The benefits to the company include goodwill, the development of a self-improvement culture, and the infusion of new ideas. Require a C grade (or better) for reimbursement, to be paid after the course is completed.

**3.** Ask vendors to have their sales and technical people make presentations and conduct in-house seminars for employees. Most good vendors will turn cartwheels at the invitation; they are looking for opportunities to cement relations with their customers. And their presentations are relevant and free.

**4.** Demand of employees that something measurable evolve from every training dollar spent. Then follow it up.

For most of us, writing checks for training is a variable expense and a painful experience. Hence training fulfills a minor or nonexistent role in our company's growth, as we focus instead on learning by old-fashioned trial and error.

My own company could have significantly blunted the trauma of our Years from Hell, had we thrown even moderate training in the direction of our managerial weaknesses.

Instead, I let the relentless pace of our sales growth leave our collective management skills behind. The managers (and I) were blindsided by the unexpected appearance of the Years from Hell.

Without training, we never had a chance.

## THE BOTTOM LINE

Training lacks the impact of learning by trial and error but comes at a fraction of the cost.

Dollars spent on training should not be considered an expense but rather an investment.

Training without follow-up isn't training. It's waste.

# 30

# COMMUNICATIONS

I DON'T LIKE the word *communications*. It's overused, abused, ambiguous, and usually a crutch.

"I'm sorry that the general ledger package for your new computer broke down. Must have been a breakdown in communications," the software vendor shrugs, as if everything is OK after this explanation. Which didn't identify the cause or resolve the problem.

I'm the first to admit that communications, whatever the hell it means, is a problem everywhere: at home, at the office, or when ordering an egg sunny-side up. But just blaming a lack of communications is not enough. We need to know more.

Is it verbal communications between peers? From-the-top-down communications? From-the-bottom-up? Is it daily operational communications between working departments or between co-workers? Is it written communications—memos, letters, newsletters? Is it telephone or fax? Is it grapevine (always an integral part of any organization's communication system)? Is it our employees' understanding, or misunderstanding, of our company's missions or goals or strategies?

Communication issues can be extremely complex or blushingly simple. One of my location managers called me to discuss a problem he was having. During the course of the conversation, he explained that the reason we had not spoken for a week was that he had been mad at me.

"And why have you been mad?" I asked.

"I forget."

Now I'm not sure who was at fault in this exchange, but if the two of us can't communicate any better than that, it is the company that ultimately will pay.

It is impossible to discuss communications without mentioning the value of listening. Business communication depends much more on the spoken word than it does on the written word, and listening is the most important part of the verbal process.

Today's successful sales folks have learned the value of listening. Everything we read today on the subject of sales stresses the importance of listening in the selling process. Our salespeople win or lose on the basis of their ability to listen and to determine their customers' needs. If they ask the right questions, listen for the response keys, and draw the correct conclusions, they usually win. If they don't, they lose. No longer must the successful salesperson be glib and articulate. No longer are the song-and-dance routines of Willy Loman an integral part of the selling process.

Communicating with employees is no different from listening to customers. The entrepreneur's job is to determine their needs and then solve their problems. Out with the songs and dances and in with listening and responding. At the same time, we should encourage our employees to learn what it takes to communicate with us.

The bigger our company becomes the more people we employ, and the more people we employ the further from the production floor we find ourselves. As our business grows and prospers, we are bound to spend less time making things happen there and in the marketplace, and more time communicating with those who do.

The communication issue where our employees are concerned is, after all, nothing more than common sense. So what if someone has a great idea, a foolproof strategy, or a better way to skin a cat? What good will it do if no one knows it? Or understands it?

We can kick off the process of improving employee communications by working from the top down. Do the employees know what is going on strategically within the company? Do they understand why we closed the Chicago office? Do they know our competitors? Our corporate mission and goals? Are they aware of the key financial aspects of the business?

In other words, are we communicating with our employees as if they were temporary clock-punchers, or do we make them feel like a permanent and integral part of the team? By communicating strategic and financial information (in language they can understand), we tell them that their enlightenment matters. At the same time we can educate them to help us improve the company.

The result? A damn large dividend at a damn small price.

And speaking of sharing financial figures, I don't understand why all of us private company folks don't. Most employees don't understand the first thing about what it takes to turn sales into earnings. They have no idea how much the company earns or what goes into the determination of profits. They don't know that 40 percent of corporate profits (in Minnesota anyway) go to income taxes, they don't know how a company can make profits and still be short of cash, and they don't understand that reinvestment of profits provides opportunities for them. By sharing our financial figures and the strategy that begets them, and then following up with education, we can better equip our employees to become the corporate citizens we want.

The ultimate goal when we decide to share financial information should not be to make all of our employees CPAs. Rather, we want them to understand what they can do to affect profitability. And, equally important, to make them care about the job they do and the company they represent.

An effective (and underused) avenue for top-down employee communications in the small, entrepreneurial company is the policy manual. (In the interest of clarity, we should have one ready to hand out the day we hire the first employee.) The policy manual serves as an ideal opportunity to formally advise new employees of exactly what we expect of them, in addition to covering our legal tracks in the process. It also provides us a chance to present the company's important strategic and cultural objectives for the first time.

We should include in this policy manual, in addition to our strategic and cultural messages, such issues as descriptions of hours to be worked, benefits, salary and performance reviews, holidays, overtime policies, vacations, severance pay policies, pension plans, and the causes for disciplinary actions and termination. Spelling out these policies in advance can save both employer and employee subsequent unpleasantries.

Most entrepreneurs do not have either a human resource or internal communications department on which to depend for top-down communications. These must come directly from us, or from somebody close to us who shares our vision. The vehicles available, in addition to the policy manual, include regularly scheduled employee meetings, memos, newsletters, and one-on-one conversations. We should utilize them all, with the up-front intent of informing our employees, not selling them. (They can tell the difference.)

Synergy is another aspect of effective communications that can be encouraged by creative leadership. Synergy is the coordination of disparate groups within the company to arrive at a sum that is greater than the individual parts. Or, more simply put, two heads are better than one, especially when those two heads are filled with complementary information.

In my company, as an example, it was imperative that the art and sales departments work closely together in designing and creating sportswear programs for our retail customers. Yet most artists have an inbred mistrust of salespeople's egos, while salespeople believe that artists suffer from overactive sensitivity genes. The result? Too often we lost the creative synergy necessary to develop our retail programs—programs that were the most important component of our product.

Following is a list of suggestions to abet the synergic process:

**1.** Require departmental heads to attend key meetings of synergic departments. (In my case, this would have meant that key members of the art department would attend designated sales meetings and vice versa.)

**2.** Require key representatives of nonsales departments to periodically accompany salespeople on customer calls.

**3.** Conduct in-house training classes designed to educate all employees on the advantages of working together synergically.

**4.** Include all key employees in strategy and planning meetings.

**5.** Spread a culture that encourages synergy throughout the company. Let your employees know, by your example, that you reward those who work together and frown on those who don't. Don't protect those lonesome outcasts who may be geniuses at whatever they do but who destroy the team as they go about it.

No discussion of communications would be complete without a mention of the annual performance review. In a perfect world, communications and feedback would be ongoing and straightforward, and there would be no need for formal performance reviews. Ours is not a perfect world, and none of us are perfect communicators. We need a formal feedback system.

Formal performance reviews should take place once a year, to be followed up six months later. The intent of these annual reviews should be to compliment the employee being reviewed as well as to correct him. They should be two-way sessions; that is, the reviewee should have the opportunity to communicate his suggestions and gripes to the reviewer. The reviewer should go to great lengths to prepare for these reviews. They are meaningful to the employees and a key to one-on-one communication success.

### THE BOTTOM LINE

Communications is the nervous system of a company, the conduit for the exchange of ideas and information.

Clear and factual communications at all levels is a necessary element of success. The entrepreneur can begin the process of assuring effective communications by making top-down communications an example of what he expects.

And lest it be forgotten, to the best listener go the communication spoils.

# 31

## COPING WITH CHANGE

CHANGE IS A constant.

Hackneyed? Maybe, but a truism we damn well better understand. And learn to deal with. And even enjoy, if we want to survive in the entrepreneurial arena.

Nowhere have the winds of change blown harder than in small business. The result is that today's successful entrepreneur must be ready to compete on a much more elevated playing field than we old-timers played on twenty years ago. Sophistication and technology have replaced sweat and determination as the primary entrepreneurial tools.

These winds of change have come from every direction, from every imaginable nook and cranny of our business. Some of that change has come in short spurts, some in long blasts. Some evolved slowly, some appeared overnight. Some changes were inevitable in the course of business evolution, others have pummeled us as punishment for getting caught with our collective hands in the cookie jar of the eighties.

A look at some of the most noticeable entrepreneurial changes of the past twenty years can give an idea of what can be expected during the next twenty:

**A Global Economy:** It is no longer only the automobile and electronics industries that have felt the pinch of offshore competition. Today even the smallest entrepreneur can no longer avoid the tentacles of foreign competition which wriggle in to steal old and loyal customers using price and quality as bait. And if you aren't competing with them you are selling to them. Or selling for them. Or purchasing from them.

So, don't fight it. Anticipate it.

And find a niche that works in spite of foreign competition. Or because of it.

**Quality:** In 1972 mediocrity was acceptable, today it is not. The trend to quality will continue to accelerate.

**Availability:** Availability, like quality, has become as important a factor as price in the customer's buying decision. The high cost of carrying inventory has necessitated the development of a host of just-in-time inventory systems.

Quicker is always better, and the majority of today's customers are willing to pay a premium for it.

**The Customer:** In 1972 salespeople hit the streets looking to write orders. Today they seek relationships. Writing the order is only a part of the sales process.

In 1972 the entrepreneur was a vendor to his good customers, today he is a partner.

**Sales Techniques:** To the best talker went the order in 1972. Today the order goes to the best listener.

Salespeople don't sell anymore. They build relationships by solving customers' problems. The sale is a by-product of that relationship.

**Management Techniques:** Entrepreneurs were dictators in 1972. This was a relatively simple management system—bark the orders and work till you drop. The entrepreneur who put in the longest hours and intimidated his employees the most usually won.

Today Peters and Blanchard and a host of believers have introduced softer, more complex, and yes, infinitely more effective management techniques. As a result, the entrepreneur who surrounds himself with the best people and learns how to empower them wins.

**Employees' (and Society's) Rights:** In 1972 the bookkeeper for the small entrepreneur also doubled as his personnel department. Today, sadly, the entrepreneur needs a trained human resources specialist to sort out all the government directives that dictate what he can and cannot do.

**A Litigious Society:** In 1972 the only lawyer you needed was the guy who filed your articles of incorporation. Today everybody has a spare litigator stashed away somewhere. The threat of impending litigation affects the way you conduct your business, its cost, and your choice of associates.

**Employee Ownership:** Who ever heard of an ESOP twenty years ago? Today everybody should consider one.

**Information:** Today, information is everywhere. It isn't expensive, and it's available to all. The advantage goes to the entrepreneur who learns how to retrieve it and use it in the shortest time.

**Government:** The environment is protected, minority rights are defended, products are tested, activities are regulated, and taxes are collected, all by a government agency somewhere. Like it or not, the heavy hand of government will continue to play an even more active role in the way business is conducted.

Damnable regulation. Inefficient, costly, and (too often) necessary. The S&L crisis proved that.

**Availability of Capital:** While finding capital has never been easy, you could usually locate what you needed in 1972 if the niche and the players were right. Not so today, with the memories and lessons of the eighties still fresh in the minds of the money lenders. Most lenders and investors were burned, and only time will heal their wounds.

Meanwhile, it is the creditless, start-up entrepreneurs who will pay the price until the invoice for that decade is paid.

**Cost of Capital:** When capital can be found, at least it's affordable. And likely to stay that way. Ten years ago money cost 20 percent or more.

**Ethics:** The greed of the eighties has soured us all. Ethics are due for a comeback, and none too soon.

## THE BOTTOM LINE

Things will never go back to the way they were. The good old days, if that's what they were, are gone forever.

Tomorrow will be an improvement over yesterday for those who learn to look at change as an opportunity.

# VI

## ORIGINS OF
## THE MOST PAINFUL
## MISTAKES

# 32

---

# HIRING

---

BY NOW, even the crustiest and most independent pantser among us must realize that our number one entrepreneurial duty is to surround ourselves with a team of superstars. If this is a fact, the importance of the hiring process becomes readily evident. Superstars are not delivered to our office by one-day air. They don't arrive on our doorstep wrapped in swaddling clothes.

Somebody's got to hire them.

Which introduces the number one rule of the number one way in which we can perform our number one chore: **The best employees surround the entrepreneur who is willing to go to the most trouble to find them.**

Hiring's no art, it's a science. And a damn sight less exciting a science than, say, oceanography or archeology. It's methodical and it's repetitive and it's a drawn-out, ho-hum, brain-dulling process that is one aggravating detail after another.

Success at the science of hiring requires rigid attention to detail and focus on the issue at hand, those proven and reliable entrepreneurial killers. If we are going to hire right, we must interview, and reinterview, and reinterview again. We must pick up the phone and check those always-exciting personal references, whose primary function in life, we soon learn, is to tell us as little as possible between rushes of glowing adjectives. We must ask the right questions, listen between the lines, and leave no lapses in time unquestioned. We must jump on the most obscure danger signals and pursue them with vigor until they are revealed as either the darkest of secrets or the deadest of ends. We must focus on the issue and beat that torrent of details to death, all the time wishing we were somewhere else—on a sales call perhaps, or walking the manufacturing floor.

Try the following exercise the next time a superstar hire is necessary and you aren't completely psyched up for the task: try attaching a dollar cost to your failure.

Assume, for instance, that you have a $10 million rapidly growing company and are shopping about for a superstar CFO. What will it cost if you hire the wrong person? The cost will equal the expense of the mistakes that are sure to follow, plus wasted training time, plus the expense of rehiring and starting all over again.

The answer, in this instance, is a minimum of a half-million dollars, a maximum of Chapter 7, and untold years of regret. I should know, it happened to me in a somewhat different form. The cost was somewhere in between, and I'll pay until the day I die. And I've no one to blame but myself. I did the hiring.

The process of hiring a superstar should proceed something like this:

**Interview 1:** Takes place in the office amid a barrage of questions, with the interviewee doing 90 percent of the talking. Immediately following the interview, begin the reference-check process, while the details are still fresh in your mind.

**Interview 2:** On neutral turf this time, maybe for breakfast or lunch. Relax the applicant, loosen him up, get a look at his social and personal side. Ask those puzzling questions that have emerged as a result of the reference checks.

**Interview 3:** If all has gone well thus far, have the applicant go through the interviewing process with several key employees who also have a stake in the success of the hire. Ask their opinions. Compare. Discuss. Listen. After all, if he isn't going to fit, it's better to find out sooner than later.

**Interview 4:** Review, negotiate, and close, if he still passes muster. And then cross your fingers. There are no guarantees in the science of hiring no matter how thorough a job is done. The odds can improve with experience and effort but failure will never disappear.

Here is a list of hiring hints to help locate that elusive superstar:

**1.** The hiring process requires you to wear two hats. The first is the hat of the detective, as you attempt to determine whether the applicant is hero or bum. The second is the salesman's hat, to be donned once the hero is located. Don't forget to prepare for the second role, and don't incorrectly assume that your company is the only, or the best, opportunity in town.

**2.** The best hires are usually the ones that are the most difficult to close. Negotiations are bound to be tense and the process drawn out. The procedure can be exhausting at the time, often to the point of evoking anger, but isn't this the kind of negotiator you eventually want on your side?

The better the applicant the more difficult he will be to sign. Winners have more options than losers. Or, stated another way, beware of the hire who signs too easily.

**3.** Try to establish some ground of commonality between the reference checks and yourself, thereby opening the door to more candid conversations.

Most references talk warily, having read horror stories of their legal liability inherent in passing public judgment on others. Look for the little things as you listen, and read between the spoken lines. Ask about the applicant's weaknesses, then multiply by a factor of five.

And remember, those references you find on the interviewee's list usually double as friends.

**4.** The best references are those the applicant doesn't list. Review the résumé, then network friends and business acquaintances to find third-party references who will talk out of school.

**5.** Look for the applicant's ability to listen as well as to speak. If he doesn't listen during an interview, he sure as hell isn't about to listen on the job.

**6.** By dissecting the motives behind the applicant's questions (and he had better ask some good ones), you can learn what it is that is important to him. What does he want to know about you? Are his questions meaningful? Sensible? Logical? Is he looking for a place to hang his hat, or does he want to make a contribution?

**7.** What research has the applicant done on you? If he comes to the interview unprepared, you are learning something about either his work habits or the depth of his desire for the job.

**8.** Favorite interviewing questions of mine:

- What are your weaknesses?
- What are your strengths?
- Why should I hire you?
- What do you want to be doing five years from now?
- What is your most significant business achievement?
- What is your biggest failure and what did you learn from it?
- What would you like to know about me and about my company?

**9.** While on the subject of questions you should ask, there are a number of questions you can't. You can't ask the applicant's age, race, religion, citizenship, or political persuasion. And you can't inquire about parental status or health.

**10.** Keep the pipeline of potential superstars full. Maintain a black book of candidates' names, even though you're not currently shopping. The list should include people you believe to be capable, and who could be lured away from their current employment. Let your employees know of the existence of the black book, so they can help keep it filled.

**11.** The good applicants will want to know exactly what the job entails, and what is expected of them. Prepare a professionally written job proposal before making your offer, a proposal that delineates everything the applicant might want to know. Include job definition, salary, bonus, perks, time frames, and your expectations.

There is an endless list of benefits that come from hiring right. The biggest? The better the employee the less time will have to be spent managing him. Instead we can spend our time in front of the customer, or on the production floor, or working with product development. Doing those things we enjoy the most and we do the best, while leaving the rest to our superstars.

Effective hiring, unlike understanding cash flow or filing tax returns, does not require a rocket scientist's IQ. There are endless books on the subject, as well as seminars, classes, and consultants ready to help locate and hire the superstar of our dreams.

With all of this assistance at our fingertips, there is no excuse for repeated failure.

Our only enemy is ourselves.

### THE BOTTOM LINE

It's difficult to put a price tag on the value of a good hire but relatively easy to attach a cost to a bad one.

Every position you fill has a related cost of failure, with the CFO at the top of the list and the sales manager not far behind.

Hiring the best employees makes the entrepreneur's life easier. Good ones don't require motivating or baby-sitting, they only need training and liberating.

# 33

# FIRING

"OK, SCHELL, I did what you said. I wined, dined, psychoanalyzed. I even had the guy's handwriting analyzed. It took a month from my life but I found my hero and hired him.

"Well, the paint on his parking space was still wet when I learned the guy was no hero, he was a goat. What do I do now?"

The weakest employees will surround the entrepreneur who procrastinates the longest when it's time to say good-bye. Once the hire is made, our responsibility in the process of collecting superstars is not over. Assuming the law of averages is alive and well, sixty days after the hire our hero may merit a fire, with all its attendant conflict. Our trusty entrepreneurial instincts will then rise up to work against us, as we put off the unpleasant deed for another six months, or at least until our performing employees form a line outside our office and let us know it is either him or them.

Which reminds me.

Ten years ago I fired a loyal, longtime employee. He was a nice person and a good friend, but the Peter Principle had been hard at work for several years. I dressed in black and did the dirty deed, two years too late for both of us. Violating firing's cardinal rule of brevity, we muttered and bumbled back and forth for three long hours, dragging out the pain.

The trauma of that firing soured me on termination for the rest of my managerial life. My head always knew when it was due, but my heart had a listening problem. Meanwhile, my friend was two years late getting on with his life, and my company was short a dozen or so good employees who might have otherwise hung around. Not to mention the loss of more customers than I want to remember and a corresponding loss of profits.

Let's face it, I doubt if even George Steinbrenner enjoys the firing process, but the timely performance of it is an integral part of our responsibility to surround ourselves with that team of superstars. If we are one of those folks whose logic is dictated by our heart and not our head, here are several arguments to help the heart reach the right decision:

**1.** Most employees know when they are underperforming. They are usually just as unhappy in their jobs as you are in having them there but are too afraid or insecure (or motivated by unemployment laws) to make the first move.

**2.** The size and frequency of opportunities available to your performing employees are adversely affected by the presence of underperforming employees on the payroll. You are doing your contributing employees a gross injustice by keeping the sluggards around.

**3.** You have an obligation to your performing team members, your shareholders, and your creditors to collect superstars, not benchwarmers.

**4.** Ease up on yourself. You are not passing judgment on the person being terminated, but rather on his behavior in that particular job. His talents, which may be many, simply lie elsewhere.

All of which will still not make the firing process the highlight of your week, but it might allow you to get an hour or two of sleep after a tough one.

Here are several tips on how to go about the unpleasant task of firing:

**1.** In business as in life, postponed problems never get any better, they only get worse. As soon as the decision is made to terminate, get on with it.

**2.** Explore alternatives. Demotion, grace periods, consultant contracts. When they don't work, have the reasons why ready. The employee will probably ask.

**3.** Arrange for outplacement services.

**4.** When firing an old-time employee or a minority, check with an attorney first.

**5.** Prepare the firing package in the same organized and documented way you prepare a hiring package. Include severance, health insurance, disposal of company car, duration of other benefits, etc.

**6.** Plan the firing itself as if it were a business meeting (which it is). Organize in advance, outline the presentation, have handouts ready. Make it as businesslike as possible, and, above all, avoid sentimentality and reminiscing. Keep emotions subdued; they only make things worse.

**7.** Don't argue. State the reasons and the facts surrounding the termination. Arguing won't change your mind and will only serve to incense the person being fired. Let him unload if he chooses— he might feel better when he's done.

**8.** Arrange the day so the firing is followed by something you enjoy, something designed to take your mind off the event. A movie, a tennis game, a jaunt with the kids.

And remember this when you start feeling sorry for yourself: It's a hell of a lot tougher on the guy across the desk.

## THE BOTTOM LINE

Firing is as important to the process of accumulating superstars as hiring.

Procrastination is the number one enemy of necessary termination. The longer firing is put off, the costlier the mistake becomes.

Don't let the heart dictate to the head in matters of termination. The entrepreneur has a responsibility to his performing employees, and the presence of underperformers in key positions violates that responsibility.

# 34

# CASH FLOW

MOST OF US can understand profit and loss statements. Layman friendly, they measure profitability and efficiency of operations over a period of time: last month, last quarter, or last year. P&Ls are history—yesterday's news—and usually include a generous sprinkling of percentages and prior-period comparisons. They can be an information overload, if we allow it.

Balance sheets are even easier to understand. Snapshots of the day on which they are prepared, they take assets (what we have), subtract liabilities (what we owe), and arrive at equity (what's left over). Balance sheets are arithmetic at its fundamental best. Like P&Ls, they also include a number of meaningful ratios—comparisons to prior periods and comparisons to budget.

As if to punish us for the relative ease of understanding P&Ls and balance sheets, the most important financial document, the cash-flow report, is also the most difficult to understand.

Like government regulations and computer manuals, the concept of cash flow, as well as the process of accounting for it, is user unfriendly to most of us nonfinancial types. Cash-flow projections are not yesterday's news or even today's. They are tomorrow's dart throw, an educated guess, as we attempt to peer beyond the present and into the murky, unpredictable future. Who really knows what lurks behind the myriad of assumptions that must be made to prepare useful cash-flow projections?

Most of the numbers used in predicting cash flow are little more than assumptions. Educated assumptions perhaps, but assumptions nevertheless. When we indulge in this voodoo art of cash-flow forecasting, we may as well consult with a fortune-teller along with our CFO, or connect a crystal ball to our computer's modem. We are, in the process, forced to conjure our best guesses for tomorrow's inventory levels, sales forecasts, interest-rate fluctuations, payable turns, projected expenses, and asset purchases. We take the results, stir them together, and before we can say hocus-pocus, we have the magic potion called projected cash flow.

Based on this combination of science and the occult, we declare ourselves ready to plan our company's future. If garbage has gone into our computations, then trash will come out. If gold goes in, wealth will emerge. Our plans for tomorrow are only as good as the assumptions we make.

Despite all these disclaimers, today's projection of tomorrow's cash flow is absolutely the most important financial report we will ever generate. It is also the most difficult to prepare. And the most undependable. Only the company with strong financial systems and capable financial employees will be able to produce accurate cash-flow reports.

Cash and the flow thereof were never a problem during National Screenprint's UPS and early Sunshine Years. Our profit growth kept up with or exceeded our sales growth, inventory was under control, and our growth was manageable, allowing our bank to treat us like any Latin American country. We got what we wanted.

Since cash wasn't a problem in those early years, we didn't take the time to track it. Besides, I was too busy watching our CFOs come and go. Any serious attempt at projecting cash flow somehow slipped through our financial reporting cracks.

Our sales would top $12 million before we made our initial attempt at tracking cash flow. The bank was asking a new set of questions in those late sunshine days, prompted by a dramatic change in our business begetting a rapidly changing balance sheet. Exploding sales in collusion with burgeoning receivables and swelling inventory will result in shrinking cash. Every time.

An accurate cash-flow forecasting system takes years to perfect. Our inability over the next several years to accurately project cash flow, and our lengthy, frustrating, and only moderately successful attempt to perfect the process, were significant contributors to the duration and severity of our Years from Hell.

Me? I couldn't put together a creditable set of cash-flow projections if my life depended on it. But I would never again hire a CFO (or controller) who hasn't had a wealth of experience in generating these projections. (The SBA can also help. Pick up a ten-page pamphlet entitled "Understanding Cash Flow" at their local office.)

Those hard-nosed turnaround guys, when they move in with six-shooters blazing to work out troubled companies, send their premier gunslingers after cash flow the minute they walk through the door. They know that cash is king.

The next time around I'll track cash flow before the ink is dry on our articles of incorporation.

### THE BOTTOM LINE

Employees and customers may be the lifeblood of a business, but cash flow is the heartbeat.

If I were a banker I would insist on receiving copies of all my client's cash-flow reports. These are the most important financial documents a company generates.

The ability to meet today's payroll and pursue tomorrow's strategies is foretold by cash-flow projections. A week should never go by without generating a fresh one, except when cash is tight, in which case every day warrants a fresh one.

# 35

## INVENTORY

MY NEXT COMPANY will accept only cash. No receivables.

My next company will employ only me. No workmen's comp.

My next company will be low-tech in a high-tech niche. Minimum risk, high potential.

And (this last one's a cinch) my next company will sell only service. No inventory.

No joke.

Aside from cheating the IRS or squealing on the Mafia, accumulating inventory is the quickest and easiest way I know to get into trouble. Excess inventory and its long list of hidden horrors are sure to hasten, and extend, anybody's Years from Hell.

We can't give inventory a golden parachute and send it out the door. Nor can we mail threatening letters and expect it to turn into cash. Bells and whistles don't go off while it sits silently on our shelf and turns yellow with age.

Inventory is our silent and deadly enemy. It just sits there, staring at us, collecting dust. And interest. Its edges get frayed from handling, counting, and auditing, while our nerves get frayed from tallying, worrying, and paying.

Yes, sometimes it disappears, but not always in the manner

intended. And sometimes it loses value, without moving so much as an inch. Or maybe it never arrives on our receiving dock in the first place and we pay for it anyway. Count the ways that inventory can shrink:

- Manufacturing spoilage
- Damage in handling
- Internal theft
- External theft
- Obsolescence
- Invoiced from vendor at price higher than our cost on the books
- Error in receiving in favor of the vendor
- Error in invoice to our customer in customer's favor
- Salesman's samples
- And more

My advice on inventory? Avoid it at all costs. In the event that you can't, here are some tips on how to minimize the negative effects of inventory on the bottom line:

**1.** An accurate and smooth MIS and paperwork flow is the number one key to handling inventory. The CFO should be responsible for ensuring that the inventory accounting system clicks. The entrepreneur is responsible for hiring the right CFO and making him accountable for managing this asset. And following up when he doesn't, if you know what I mean.

**2.** Make the director of purchasing a vice president. Hire a superstar for this position, and don't underestimate the requirements and responsibilities of the job.

Then give him the clout he needs to deal with the sales department—who will be forever glued to purchasing's door, screaming for more inventory.

**3.** If you don't assume direct accountability for inventory yourself, at least make it your personal priority to oversee progress or failure in achieving the goals that are established. If your employees, especially those in purchasing and sales, know that your eyes are glued to inventory levels, then inventory awareness will become a part of your corporate culture.

**4.** Take quarterly inventories at the very least. Monthly or bimonthly if possible. The trail gets too cold when the counts are made only once or twice a year.

**5.** Divide the inventory into small, manageable pieces, allowing for easier tracking and quicker reference. This will also make inventory listings more user friendly, especially for the sales department.

Then get involved in setting minigoals for those manageable pieces. Acknowledge those responsible when the minigoals are met; close the door and have frank discussions concerning cloudy futures when they are not.

**6.** Assign direct accountability for every dollar in the inventory. Or keep that accountability for yourself, if you are so inclined. In any event, make a superstar responsible, for all of the company to observe. Devise bonus plans that reward those responsible for achieving inventory-turn goals.

**7.** Identify your most-wanted-to-dump inventory, and make heroes of the salespeople who sell it. Financially reward them and stroke them and publicly appreciate them.

**8.** Make sure there are good employees at the handling corners: receiving and shipping. Train and cross-train those employees thoroughly, not only on their own job but on related bookkeeping functions as well. Most inventory shrinkage problems can be identified and resolved at the bookkeeping level.

**9.** Bankers don't like inventory hits that accumulate but aren't taken. They not only ruin the latest financials, they are tough on credibility. Don't postpone taking the painful write-downs, and take them in the year they occur. Postponing them may rescue the current year's P&L, but the pain will eventually come—compounded.

**10.** Anticipate increased computer and inventory handling needs at least two years in advance. It takes a year or more to spec and purchase hardware and software and start up a new inventory system. Don't wait until the current system is overloaded.

**11.** There is a wide variety of just-in-time vendor systems in use today. Study them and adopt whatever applies. Admittedly, most are difficult to adapt to the small entrepreneurial company that is typically lacking in clout with its vendors. But you can learn from the just-in-time process, and big advances in inventory handling come largely through a string of small but continuous improvements.

**12.** And finally, when in doubt, cancel the damn order. Your vendors will scream, but it's better than eating the stuff.

There is some good news on the subject of inventory. The opportunities to improve profitability by the efficient handling of it are endless. Inventory isn't gray, like marketing, or steeped in hypothesis, like sales. It is there to touch and feel and count, and the impact of inventory exchanged for cash is instantaneous. And oh, so pleasurable.

If you are one of the few who have learned how to handle inventory properly, this can only invite further success. Availability of product is everything in these days of on-time delivery expectations. Those who are able to provide inventory immediately upon request, without shrinking it, and ship it immediately, without losing it, can write their own ticket.

And one final piece of good news, if you are into handling inventory for a living: you won't have me to compete with.

### THE BOTTOM LINE

Unlike cash, inventory collects dust, not interest.

Unlike real estate, inventory's natural tendency is to shrink, not inflate.

Unlike equipment, inventory's presence does not improve efficiency.

Unlike receivables, you can't go to court and exchange inventory for cash.

Handle inventory with care, or don't handle it at all. It is the most dangerous asset you own.

# 36

## EXPENSE CONTROL

THERE ARE ONLY three ways to increase profitability: 1) increase revenues; 2) increase margins; and 3) decrease expenses.

The first two are exercises in enjoyment for most of us. The third is not.

Pursuit of the first two is optional. Pursuit of the third is not.

Not too many years ago, strict control of expenses was an option as well. But the effects of global competition and today's advances in technology have changed the rules of the game. No longer are we able to include fat in the cost of our product. Today, expense control is a way of life.

How about you? Don't you get style-over-substance shivers whenever you pull into an office parking lot filled with the Mercedeses and Jaguars of management, then enter a reception area replete with splashing waterfalls and original paintings? Doesn't it make you wonder why they are there? And for whom they are there?

And who is it that pays for those cascading waters? The customers? The employees? Somebody has to pay.

Whenever I get hit by a blast of style over substance, I am

reminded of Wal-Mart, arguably this country's greatest corporate success story of the past twenty years. Our sales people who called on the Bentonville, Arkansas, retailer always came back with tales of linoleum floors and metal desks and employees who took pride in keeping their expenses down.

No Mercedes could be found in Sam Walton's parking spot. He drove an old pickup. "What am I supposed to haul my dogs around in," he was reported to have replied to a curious reporter, "a Rolls-Royce?"

Even in the safest of niches, the windows of opportunity are only wide open for short periods of time. Competitors attack quickly, using updated technology and cheap labor as weapons, and are in front of our customers with look-alike products and services in the space of a few months. Price suddenly becomes an increasingly important factor in the customer's decision to purchase, and the product burdened with the fewest expenses has the lead. It is poised to get its foot in our customer's door.

Effective control of expenses requires a corporate culture that recognizes the natural tendency of costs, like hot air, to rise when uncontrolled. As Wal-Mart has proved, a strong expense-control culture must be born at, and maintained from, the desk at the top. Like Sam Walton, every entrepreneur must practice frugality. The penalty when he doesn't is soaring costs and plummeting profitability. As well as the demise of his own credibility.

Just as a successful product needs a champion behind it, so a successful expense-control program needs a champion. A bulldog, remember? In this case the bulldog must be either the entrepreneur or an extremely strong CFO supported by him.

In addition to the entrepreneur and the CFO, the purchasing agent is an important and unsung player in controlling expenses. The cost-controlling role of the purchasing agent, along with the depth of his inventory responsibilities, makes his position one of the most pivotal, overlooked, and unappreciated jobs in our company.

Once an expense-containment culture and its bulldog champion are in place, the next step is to introduce a zero-base budgeting program. Zero-basing requires that we begin each year's annual budget categories at absolute zero, from which point every budgeted dollar must be justified, old as well as new. That mindless standby of budgeting expenses by making across-the-board percentage increases for inflation is no longer acceptable.

While the onus for the establishment and maintenance of an ongoing no-nonsense expense culture remains solely upon us, the responsibility for each zero-based expense category should be delegated to the people who are in the best position to control it. These people must be included in the original budgeting process and then held accountable for staying within their designated budgets.

Success in remaining within the boundaries of budgeted dollars should be measured and subsequently rewarded. Failure should be similarly measured and dealt with in a manner designed to reinforce our stance on the subject of expense containment. In this way, the seeds of an expense culture, sown earlier, are reaped.

Here's a suggestion for a short-term expense-control exercise that will open every entrepreneur's eyes to the need for action. For a designated period of time (six months at least), route every vendor purchase order over your desk. It's amazing what you will learn about how your money is being spent as you OK that never-ending stream. Additionally, the exercise by itself will cut expenditures: scrutiny from above is the best auditor of them all.

The 80/20 rule (which seems to turn up everywhere) is hard at work within the individual expense categories. Eighty percent of wasted expense dollars can be found in 20 percent of the P&L categories. The wages and salary category is the largest and usually the most heavily infested with waste. It is also the most sacrosanct, and attempts to zero-base it will not be greeted with ticker-tape parades by most employees. The benefits category is another sacred but inflated collection of old expenses, and no audit is complete that doesn't peek into its hallowed closets.

All of which is not to say expenses shouldn't be challenged in all categories, large or small. There are quick and easy dollars to be found by rooting around in such overlooked compartments as utilities, travel and entertainment, insurance, and the compost heap of them all, the miscellaneous account.

I always had trouble controlling my company's expenses. Not

because I was a big spender. I wasn't. My CFO hiring problems were a significant contributor, along with my own shortcomings when it came to attention to detail, focus, and follow-up.

Effective expense control requires attention to all of these.

## THE BOTTOM LINE

In today's competitive times, effective control of expenses is no longer an option, it is a necessity. That need becomes more pronounced with each passing year, as competitors emerge from every corner of the globe.

A culture that rewards frugality must begin at the top, and the champion must be either the entrepreneur or an effective and strongly supported CFO.

Zero-based budgeting is an integral part of controlling expenses. Accountability for making zero-basing work must be in the hands of those who spend the money, as opposed to those who account for it.

# 37

## FOCUS

YOU NAME IT, and in the interest of keeping up with the latest in business trends, I've read it: Peters and Drucker and Blanchard and Iacocca and McCormack and Ouchi, to mention a few. Little has escaped my wandering eye.

I've tried to use the best of the tidbits garnered from those readings in raising my own company from toddlerhood to adulthood. When I returned to my office after my latest skirmish with a new idea, theory, attitude, or resolution, the memos would fly and the meetings would multiply as I strived mightily to kickstart my latest revelation.

On their part, my employees would brace themselves in advance of the onslaught, having been duly warned that Jim was reading Peters again, or Jim was going to a two-day conference on quality circles. The Fad-of-the-Month Club was about to reconvene. They knew.

And right on cue, I would MBWA (Peters: Manage By Walking Around), strategize, form committees, or empower people. And while I was so occupied, our invoices would go out late, or our receivables would stretch out for another ten days, or a foreboding chunk of inventory would appear as if from nowhere. My blockbuster idea would then flop at the box office, and back I would go to resolving the latest crisis.

Great ideas Peters and his contemporaries had, revolutionary sometimes, and applicable to everyone. But they needed a manager—a professional manager—to put them to use. A manager capable of pursuing, and dogging, and sticking with those great ideas until they became permanently encased in the framework of the organization. A manager possessing an abundance of drive (like the majority of us), motivation (like the majority of us), and focus (well, two out of three isn't so bad).

Unfortunately, two out of three isn't enough. Without focus, any progress we make will only be partial, any advancement only temporary. Strategic and structural changes don't take place without focus. Cultures aren't altered without focus. The important long-term problems never get resolved without focus.

*Webster's* defines *focus* as "to fix or settle on one thing; to concentrate." For business purposes we should expand that definition to "the relentless pursuit of a project until it is completed in accordance with plan."

I hired my presidential replacement in the fall of 1989. It took the two of us an hour or so to identify and prioritize our ten biggest problems, and another few hours to outline a general plan by which to resolve all ten. So why do I need this guy? I wondered after we had finished. I could have done this alone.

It didn't take him long to justify his presence. That man could focus. I mean he was relentless. Of all the differences between him (a pedigreed professional manager) and me (a bona fide entrepreneur)—and there were many—the most noticeable was his ability to focus on whatever project he chose to pursue. Distractions that would pull me away from pet projects for days were no more than minor inconveniences to him. No matter how drab the project, no matter how serious the crisis, he would burrow forward, a mole on a mission, chipping and digging relentlessly, never losing ground.

A phone call from the plumber could distract me for hours. Plumbers never got through to him.

The professional managers of this world know that the ability to focus pays dividends. They have learned that it is far better to solve one problem forever than to have three in various stages of irresolution.

## THE BOTTOM LINE

The problem-solving equation involves three steps: identifying the issue, planning its resolution, and focusing on the solution until the issue is resolved. Without focus, the first two are wasted effort.

Identifying and planning are intellectual exercises and usually accomplished in short, intense bursts. An entrepreneur's dream.

Focus requires patience, attention to detail, concentration, an organized and adhered-to agenda, and a dogged attention span over long periods of time. An entrepreneur's nightmare.

# 38

## STRATEGY
## AND PLANNING

WE EITHER MAKE things happen or things happen to us. Most of us prefer the former when it comes to managing our business. Too many of us fall victim to the latter.

National Screenprint's unwritten and unidentified strategy in our first ten years of existence was to provide screenprinting services for sporting goods dealers. By the time the early eighties arrived, in addition to our reliable but slow-growth sporting goods niche, we had drifted into a new, potentially larger market: screenprinted sportswear products for a variety of local retail and wholesale customers.

Shortly thereafter we made yet another unplanned strategic change, as we entered the national retailing market. Bloomingdale's and Marshall Field and Wal-Mart became our customers. Our sales skyrocketed along with our inventory, receivables, and the unrelenting pressure on our thin and inexperienced management resources.

We were unprepared for the flood of new business that resulted. Short of management depth and financial strength, we also lacked state-of-the-art manufacturing equipment and the sophisticated internal systems necessary to support our sales.

There was nothing in our past to indicate we would be experiencing those tumultuous times. No advance notices. Our new markets and new customers simply appeared one day, like an unannounced visitor. We spent the next eight years trying to catch up.

One of the advantages of entrepreneuring is that it is possible, allowable, even encouraged, for such ninety-degree strategic transpositions to occur with little or no warning. This is our entrepreneurial birthright, and most of us wouldn't have it any other way. We enjoy stumbling into those new niches, and thrive on the appearance of sudden change and instant opportunity.

But how many of us enjoy coming to work every day unsure of where we're headed? Or how we're going to get there?

"Ready, fire, aim," Peters calls it.

National Screenprint's strategy and planning in those early years took place in my bed in the wee morning hours, before I left for work. Oh, we had annual managers' meetings and unofficial Saturday-morning roundtable discussions and shared our visions over a few beers now and then. But corporate strategy was locked somewhere in the back of my head, for only me to know. Planning was short term or not at all, usually nothing more than a series of knee-jerk reactions to yesterday's events.

We changed all that about the time the consultant illustrated to me that our eight key managers were strategically off in eight different directions. It was on that day I learned that strategy and planning could no longer be confined in my own head. There is a time and place, and an organized procedure for the incubation of strategy and planning. This procedure is necessary to organized growth and can even be entrepreneurially enjoyable, if pursued in an orderly fashion.

All of us have a strategy for our company, whether we know it or not, whether we articulate it or not. The trick is to define it and refine it by including input from key employees, consultants, directors, and mentors. Then, once accomplished, we can publish it and publicly commit our company to it and share it with those who are about to make it happen.

Strategy, loosely defined, is who we are and what we wish to be. The following questions must be answered to properly identify corporate strategy:

- What are the markets we pursue and wish to pursue?
- What are the products (or services) we make and wish to make?
- What capabilities do we need to service these markets and offer these products and/or services?
- What results do we expect from our activities?

The act of answering these questions and determining our strategy requires a substantial degree of organized daydreaming. (And what does a true entrepreneur enjoy more?) The strategic process requires that we first identify where we are today and then barrage the present with visions and ideas. Then sort them out and keep the best.

The next step after determining where we want to go is to find the quickest and easiest route to get there—the planning part of the strategic process. The daydreaming ends and the application begins, as we attempt to commit our available resources to our new plan.

Thus strategy and planning formulation follows an organized process. The process includes: 1) the initial assembling of facts and ideas in advance of the strategic meeting; 2) meeting as a formulating and decision-making group; 3) organizing the results into black and white statements and plans; 4) implementing the plans; and 5) officially following up six months later.

The toughest part of the process is number four, implementing the plans. Converting ideas into action. Melding reality with supposition, operations with vision.

The key to successful implementation is employee involvement. The more the merrier, the implementation rule goes, since our employees are the folks who will be doing most of the work once implementation time arrives. Effective employee involvement requires communication from us on our goals and objectives and training by us on the strategic and planning process. Our employees must know what we have planned, what we expect the results to be, and how they can contribute. They must understand where we are going, and why it is important we get there.

Effective strategy and planning does not happen on its own. It is brought about through the conduct of a formal process.

Here are some tips on how to make that process work:

**1.** A full-blown strategy and planning meeting should be held once a year, possibly twice if finances and opportunity permit. The first meeting should be dedicated to formulation, the second to review and follow-up.

**2.** Include as many key people in the strategy and planning process as possible. Key employees have meaningful visions, too—especially the superstars. Additionally, it is they who will be overseeing much of the implementation. The earlier in the process they become involved, the better the chances for success.

**3.** Gather information and suggestions and ideas in advance of the first strategy and planning meeting, by soliciting your employees' contributions. Distribute an outline in advance giving those attending ample time to consider everything on the agenda.

The key to a successful strategy and planning meeting (or any meeting, for that matter): Be long on preparation and short on surprises. Give the attendees plenty of time to ponder the issues.

**4.** Meet off-site for at least two days. Get away from the phones and the family. Have the meeting over a weekend, if the logistics of running the company would interfere with the attendees' involvement.

**5.** Find an outsider familiar with the strategy and planning process to facilitate the meeting. Do not attempt to be your own facilitator. Your mind should be free to consider content and not style. Additionally, your presence at the podium will detract from the frankness and openness of many of your employees.

**6.** Encourage a no-holds-barred atmosphere. Anything goes and everything is fair game.

**7.** Strategies and plans are not forever, particularly in a rapidly changing entrepreneurial environment that, today more than ever, favors the fleet of foot. Strategies and plans must be fashioned from elastic, not steel. Be sure to retain the capability to turn on a dime.

**8.** Strategic results and operational plans should be put to paper and shared with all employees. The act of publishing strategies and plans legitimizes the process and helps to make everyone accountable for success.

**9.** There is a wealth of information at the library on the planning and strategic process. Unfortunately, most of it is geared to Fortune 500 companies and is written by folks long on theory and short on small business applications. The ideas and the basics are there, however, to adapt to entrepreneurial needs.

The determination of strategy and the planning that follows work best as democratic processes, and increased employee involvement improves the chance for success. There will come a time, however, when the democratic process stalls, a time when the tough strategic questions require a tiebreaker. Or maybe a veto.

This is the time to remember that, while our team of employees may have laid our strategic and planning foundation, the superstructure belongs to us. (Review the guarantee on the bank loan for further evidence.)

We have a right to be the ultimate tiebreaker where the direction of the company is concerned. We have a right to enact the ultimate veto.

Do not be afraid to do either.

### THE BOTTOM LINE

Strategy is determining what you want to be.

Planning is developing the best route to get there.

An orderly and dependable future awaits those who employ proactive strategy and planning, leaving plenty of opportunity for entrepreneurial detours along the way.

The proactive process includes a formal strategy and planning meeting involving key employees, while you retain the entrepreneurial right to break ties and to veto.

# 39

## CONFLICT

## AVOIDANCE

I WAS FRESH out of college, primed to go the business route but obligated to the U.S. Air Force. My first assignment was a small base in Oregon, where I was assigned to manage an office of thirty-five military and civilian employees.

The United States was not at war back in 1959, but I soon discovered that two of my female employees were. I decided to resolve their disagreement the only way I knew at the time. I confronted it. Head on.

Second lieutenants, I know now, have been shot in the back for less.

Nellie, Dorothy, and I sat down, with me in the middle. "All right," I opened confidently, warming to the task, "what seems to be the problem?"

Whoosh. A hurricane hit the mainland. Fifteen minutes went by in what seemed like a week. By the time our problem-solving meeting had finished, what had been deep dislike before was now undying hate. A police action had escalated to war.

And I was a dishrag. My first official attempt at conflict resolution had ended in dismal failure. I was to be managerially scarred for life.

I have since learned that there is a direct correlation between the ascending levels of professional management and the degree of conflict to be faced. The higher one ascends in the management arena, the more intense the conflict becomes. The stakes in these upper levels become increasingly important and the antagonists more skilled at conflict. And more dangerous.

We all have our character flaws. Some we can work on and improve, others we can't. Attitudes toward conflict are difficult, if not impossible, to change. Either we enjoy it or we don't. Either we handle it gracefully or we don't.

Oh, we can force ourselves to face conflict and in some cases even get to the point where we can survive a heavy dose of it without requiring sedation. But those of us who are turned off by its presence will forever cringe in its presence, as the rush of adrenaline chokes our arteries and sends a cascade of blood to the brain. Reason once more will elude us, and our company pays the price.

I tried for thirty years to overcome my intense dislike for conflict, but even today I tend to look the other way when my neighbor wants to discuss why our dog prefers his lawn to mine. But, like arthritis and insomnia, conflict aversion has become a part of my life. It is here to stay.

I have a good friend who is Mr. Manager-On-The-Rise for his Fortune 500 employer. A true professional, judging from the rapidity of his climb in their corporate ranks. He was recently transferred to a new position within his company—new region, new office, new town. Big promotion.

On his first day, my friend found what he was looking for: the biggest and best conflict within his new managerial fiefdom. This particular conflict involved two office cliques, one clique led by Mr. X, the other heeling to Mr. Y. X and Y had little use for each other, and their cliques followed dutifully in their wakes, wasting everybody's time and energy, as well as sapping company profits. It was obvious to my friend that the behavior of X and Y stood in the way of his success—and his annual bonus—unless something was done.

He wasted no time.

By 11:00 that morning X and Y were in his office. "Gentlemen," my friend began, "the three of us have a problem and no one is leaving until it's resolved. Or until one or both of you are no longer employed here," he added.

They didn't make it home for dinner. They did resolve the problem.

Now I ask you, does that sound like a great way to start a day? A new job? An entire afternoon and on into the evening with nothing but heavy-duty conflict. My friend ate it up and resolved a huge problem in the process. He also went on to resolve many more huge problems over the next year and quickly put his region at the head of the corporate class.

He is the same guy who sends a steak back if it isn't cooked right. Or argues over a line call until his tennis opponent backs down. Or returns a doodad that doesn't perform to his expectations. I swear, this guy not only likes conflict, he thrives on it.

Good thing. He's surrounded with it every moment of his managerial day.

Professional managers, my friend's success has proved to me, must also be professional conflict resolvers. Which is damn tough to do when you don't like to face it in the first place.

### THE BOTTOM LINE

The meek may inherit the earth, but they will never qualify for the Managers' Hall of Fame.

# 40

# CRISIS

# MANAGEMENT

OK, I'LL ADMIT it, I always loved a good crisis. The bigger the crisis, the more excited I got. After all, a crisis would give us the opportunity to marshal our forces and the juices would begin to flow. More important, my pantser genes would rise to the surface, and I could get the hell out of the office.

Why, it got to the point where I loved our crises so much we'd plan parties around the best ones. Burgers for lunch and a beer after the trucks were gone. Our newsletter would loudly proclaim this latest victory over the process of planning. Everyone would be proud, and we would all look forward to the next one.

God, those crises were fun.

Never mind that we could never balance the packing list with the manifest when it was time for the last postcrisis truck to depart. Never mind that our printing spoilage would reach new all-time highs. Never mind that our quality on that particular job was the pits, and that our retail customer, always looking for a way to lower his costs, would charge us back for our crisis-induced sloppiness to the tune of the national debt. Never mind that each crisis required more after-the-fact shoveling out than a Minnesota snowfall.

God, those crises were expensive.

Planning is the archenemy of the crisis. The more intense the plans, the less intense the crisis. But it seems I was always too busy resolving today's crisis to find time to make the plans to avoid tomorrow's.

All of which is not to suggest that every crisis can be avoided. It can't. Random events will take their inevitable toll, no matter how thoroughly we plan. But there must be some organized methodology behind our crisis management other than flipping burgers or pouring beer.

And speaking of random events, that reminds me of politics and the president of the United States. Everyone knows the president must be the consummate crisis manager. After all, who has bigger crises? Or more of them?

Here are the rules the president is supposed to follow when his latest crisis unfolds:

### CRISIS MANAGEMENT IN THE OVAL OFFICE

- Be steady. That's what Americans most want from their president, and what adversaries most respect.
- Don't get captured by the crisis. History is full of presidents who have been obsessed with a crisis. Stick to vacation plans and regular schedules. (Ouch. I always loved cutting a vacation short to get back to a good crisis.)
- Don't act until you must. Rash decisions based on bad information are the biggest dangers in a crisis.
- Talk, talk. Use the telephone to take charge and coordinate strategy directly with other heads of state. (Talk, talk? Not me. Do, do. The entrepreneurial way.)

If you want living, breathing examples of crisis management from which to learn, tune in to CNN. Our politicians, whoever they might be, are usually there, crisis-managing away, for all the world to watch.

Of course, a bit more planning on the front end might help.

## THE BOTTOM LINE

Planning on the front end of a prospective crisis is preferable to sweating on the back end of an existing one.

Ongoing crisis-rewarding behavior only serves to instill a crisis-acceptance culture in the employees.

Effective crisis management requires patience, planning, and focus. Entrepreneurial enemies, all three.

# 41

## THE PETER
## PRINCIPLE

SOONER OR LATER the Peter Principle goes to work on us all. For me, it was at around $15 million in sales that my manager fuel ran out. I peaked. Like Reagan in 1985, or Gorbachev in 1991.

We all have our limitations, which doesn't make us rotten terrorist pigs. We are simply in the wrong job at the wrong time.

How many managers would George have to Steinbrenner before he realized why the Yankees don't win baseball championships anymore? The rest of the world knows he should stick to doing deals and buying continents, and forget trying to win baseball games. Why doesn't he?

And the same thing goes for the rest of us whose team is currently underachieving. Take a look at our role in the muddle. The buck stops here, like Harry once said.

This is basic logic I'm talking here. If things aren't working, start looking at the top. The catch, especially for folks like George, is the introspection part—their egos can't stand the strain. They can't, or they won't, admit there is someone else who could do the job. Better.

We alone are accountable for leading our company. There are

many facets to that responsibility, the foremost of which is to assure that the right people are in the right positions.

When they aren't, it's up to us to replace those who can't perform.

Especially when it's us.

## THE BOTTOM LINE

Everything starts at the top.
    And ends there, too.

# VII

## CAREER

## DECISIONS

# 42

---

# ENTREPRENEUR OR
# MANAGER?

---

THE GREAT REVELATION finally came to me in the fall of 1988. Minneapolis was at its golden best that first week in October. Even the years from hell, now in their second year, could not blunt the regenerative power of Minnesota's autumn sun.

National Screenprint was in the midst of another of our frequent and glorious crises. This particular crisis allowed us to employ one of our favorite maneuvers, the renowned "packing in the parking lot" trick. This old standby dictated that we throw every employee in the company, from president to bookkeeper, at the crisis du jour. The ploy rarely failed, and rain or snow were its only natural enemies.

We packed feverishly throughout the day. Finally, as the late afternoon sun blinked its chilly farewell, the last box was packed. The semitrailers were filled and ready to roll. The scent of victory was everywhere.

All the employees had returned to their offices except for me. I wandered aimlessly through the parking lot, enjoying the remaining fumes of the day, celebrating another victory over the process of planning.

As I shuffled, both of my feet became tangled in a piece of

polypropylene packing liner. My head and shoulders plummeted earthward, while my feet remained implanted in the plastic, which was going nowhere. The journey earthward seemed to take forever. On the way down, I can remember wondering if something like this had ever happened to Iacocca.

My thoughts were interrupted by impact. My forehead, palms, and right knee joined forces, offering only token resistance to the onrushing asphalt.

When I awoke, the Great Revelation appeared. "You ain't Iacocca, Schell, and never will be." I struggled to my feet, picked the gravel from my palms and forehead, and vowed to change my life.

It was time to hire a professional manager.

It was about time. I ultimately found the right person, and my only regret is that I didn't do it earlier.

But let's face it, I had failed. Thrown in the towel. No minor failure here, we're talking a major disappointment of career-sized proportions. I was a managerial flop. A washout. A dud. It wasn't that I hadn't tried. There was just too much to change.

Enter frazzled, beat-up entrepreneur and wise, venerable doctor.

Entrepreneur speaks while reclining on couch. "Doc, I busted my butt trying to make the transition. Read all the right books, attended all the dull seminars, hired CFOs by the truckload." Sniffling entrepreneur pauses to wipe tear from cheek as venerable doctor puffs on gnarled pipe.

"But nothing happened. Oh, my company changed some, but not all for the better. But I didn't change. Not one iota. All those idiosyncrasies that make me, well, creative and cute as my wife likes to say, hung around like lint on a navy blue suit." Doc hands entrepreneur a fresh box of Kleenex.

"Let's face it, I tried. And I failed. F-a-i-l-e-d. I'm the scum of the earth. Help me, Doc. My ego's shot to hell."

Wise, venerable doctor nods, repacks pipe amid shower of ashes.

"Son, some make it, but most don't," he spoke softly. "The lucky ones learn early on that the transition is out of their league.

Then they go out and hire themselves a president. Let him do the managing." Doctor gazes sagely out window.

"I'm not saying it's impossible to make the transition," he went on. "All you have to do is change a few dozen lifelong traits that go into making you what you are."

Doctor sucks in deep breath and relights his pipe. "Unfortunately, you're one of the majority who couldn't make the change. You've learned too late that running a five-million-dollar business isn't in the same universe as managing a twenty-five-million-dollar company."

He pauses, adjusts spectacles.

"But what the hell, so what if you succeeded at becoming that manager? Is that what you really want to do with the rest of your life? Are the changes you must make in the best interests of your employees, your shareholders, your family, and you? Or can your time be better spent doing something else?

"Think about it," he winks at wide-eyed entrepreneur. "So what if you aren't a professional manager when you grow up. There's a lot of good folks who aren't. And most don't have the cards stacked as high against them as you do. It's not un-American to fail, you know. Jose Canseco fails two-thirds of the time, and Joe Montana and Michael Jordan upwards of half.

"The important thing is, does your wife still think you're creative and cute, and do your kids still call to wish you happy Father's Day?"

Entrepreneur nods, faint smile crossing his lips.

"So what's your problem?"

## THE BOTTOM LINE

Like the venerable doctor said, "Some folks make it, but most folks don't."

The smart entrepreneur recognizes his limitations, and hires someone to take his place (preferably in advance of the Years from Hell).

# 43

## PRIVATE OR PUBLIC?

LIKE MOST WHO have spawned modestly successful companies, at one time I too eyed the golden egg of going public. The lure of liquidity is a friendly beacon to those of us who have never had enough liquid assets to pay cash for a lawnmower. I have often wondered, however, just how many of those who crossed the public line look back on their private days with more than a little remorse.

How in the hell, I wonder, do those public CEOs find the time to:

- fulfill incessant SEC regulations?
- respond to stockbroker queries?
- placate or fight dissident shareholders?
- keep skittish shareholders happy?
- invent creative ways to keep price/earnings multiples high?
- fight hostile takeovers?
- respond to media needs?

and still attend to such incidental tasks as solving employee problems, producing quality products, and taking care of customers?

I can tell you this, I would have severe mental problems resulting in violent and unpredictable behavior if I had to listen to Mr. Dissident Shareholder tell me that I should take on additional debt with which to pay cash dividends, because he is unhappily saddled with dusty shares of my company that are currently underperforming, in his opinion (please have your attorney contact my attorney, thank you very much).

Give me a break, oh dissident one. If my company's stock is underperforming, then sell it. Hence the word public. Take your beating and start a company of your own with the leftovers. Make a better widget yourself. That's America.

In the process, maybe we can both save our company some legal fees and be responsible for directing an attorney or two into making his living the old-fashioned way. Meanwhile, I have production schedules to meet, new products to research, and employees to train. A business to run.

And here's another one that kills me.

I once was a member of a group of twelve CEOs, kind of a share-your-woes support group. All were small-company folks like me. We traded problems, suggestions, solutions, and ideas. Meetings were monthly, and the networking that evolved was well worth the time. Four of the group were CEOs of public companies, the other eight came from the private side.

One of the public CEOs, a restaurant franchiser, had yet to turn a profit in the three years since his public offering. At one of our monthly meetings he passed on the news that his red-inked company was kicking off a second restaurant franchise. New theme, new menus, new decor, new advertising, new everything. This fresh venture would require several years to get into the black, he informed us.

"Whoa!" we private guys counseled in unison. "Three years you've been open for business, and have yet to record one drop of black ink. Achieve some earnings first, before digesting something new."

"Pull your collective heads out," responded our public counterparts, also in unison. "Our public charge is not earnings, but shareholder value, as measured by the stock market price. The higher the price, the more the shareholder value. And past earning history does not drive stock prices higher. Sex drives stock prices higher."

"Sex?" we asked, in our supreme ignorance.

"Yes, sex. Expectations of what is to come. Our job is to get them excited. Flash them some flesh and lure them to the dance floor. The market will take care of the rest."

And off into the world of sex went the restaurant king. He temporarily excited his shareholders, old and new, with visions of riches to come. His new restaurant franchise lasted a year and a half. By the time I left the group, he was looking for a third franchise to replace his recently failed second one.

This scenario seems ass-backward to me. I'll take earnings over anticipation any day. A bird in the hand, like my mother used to say, is always worth two in the bush.

And, as if selling sex isn't enough, those public CEOs must also contend with their corporate version of the Magna Carta, the quarterly earnings report. Those frightened and paranoid CEOs must make their long-term decisions based on not-always-so-relevant short-term documents, as legions of unhappy shareholders wait menacingly in the wings with their hangman's nooses poised and ready.

Not for me those plans and strategies that must be forgotten, those accounting practices that must be creatively altered, those customers who must be put on hold, in the name of the quarterly earnings reports.

Not for me those foreboding white papers. I want to make my decisions based on what is best for the future of my company, not on a shareholder's opinion that our last quarter's earnings report isn't up to his expectations.

Business is tough enough without dragging around the leg irons of shareholders and the shackles that go with them. I'll take usually predictable debt and sometimes unpredictable bankers over always unpredictable shareholders.

Anytime.

## THE BOTTOM LINE

Notwithstanding the lure of liquidity and interest-free cash, public-company CEOs are required to spend too much time with shareholders and stockbrokers and media, and not enough time with products and customers and employees.

If that isn't enough, the pall of quarterly earnings reports hangs over every decision the public CEO must make.

Private will always be preferable to me.

# VIII

## SELLING
## THE BUSINESS

# 44

---

# THE PROCESS

---

IS THIS AS good as it gets, we ask, when the business of business is no longer fun? When the challenge is gone, and each day feels the same? When the rest of the world continues to pass us by as we sit in the office glued to our chair? The same leather chair, interfacing with the same good people, going through the same routine that has been the story of the past twenty years.

And finally we swallow hard, realizing it is time for a new direction. A new direction for our company and a fresh start for us. We take the plunge. We put our company, our lifetime investment, up for sale.

And now, a whole new set of problems—and opportunities—are about to evolve. Problems and opportunities we've never faced before and will never face again. Within the space of the next six months we are about to reshape our lives.

Where do we begin?

The process goes something like this:

### The Commitment to Sell

Once the sales process is in motion, there will be occurrences that will be difficult to retract. Expenses are about to be incurred, employees alienated, and a host of presumptions—some right, some wrong—will be made by vendors, customers, and employees. The tongues of the industry will wag.

A decision to sell once made and later canceled is not good for the company, the employees, or the entrepreneur. (Consider a ballplayer trade that falls through. How does the ballplayer feel about the people who wanted him traded?) Hence it must be a commitment to sell that is made, not a decision to be reviewed later. Decisions can be reversed, commitments cannot.

Seller's remorse is a genetic entrepreneurial emotion that comes with the turf of making lifetime investments and then deciding to sell them. The path of every small business broker is littered with shattered deals that have fallen apart when a wave of seller's remorse overcame the entrepreneur. Once the business broker is hired, you can bet his first efforts will be to determine whether or not the entrepreneur's commitment is irrevocable and fixed. He wants to be sure the answer will be yes when he puts what he considers to be the right proposal on the seller's table.

Unsure of your commitment to sell? Doubts about the depths of your seller's remorse? Then talk to those who have sold their companies before. Ask them of the pros and cons, of the throes of entrepreneurial withdrawal, of life away from the center of the action. Accountants, attorneys, or business brokers can lead you to the people who have been there before.

If you need an unbiased estimate of what the company is worth before making a commitment to sell, hire a certified business appraiser. For $4,000 to $10,000 the appraiser can save you the trouble of going through the selling process only to determine the value of your business is less that you are prepared to accept.

However you make up your mind, be sure the commitment is secure and fixed before moving on to the next step.

## Write a Corporate Résumé

The next step, even before hiring a broker, is to compose a corporate résumé. Its purpose is twofold. First, it will be used by the business broker for background material as he prepares his sales package. Second (and more important), the résumé can be available as down-the-road evidence of honesty and good intent, in the event of after-the-sale litigation or arbitration. The résumé should be accurate and truthful, and just as forthcoming about the company's risks and weaknesses as it is about the opportunities and strengths.

Yes, *risks* and *weaknesses*. Years from now, when litigation is either threatened or real (and the odds favor it), you can pull out that tattered old résumé and illustrate your intent to alert the buyer to whatever your company's shortcomings were at the time. A frankly written corporate résumé can return the investment of time it took to create many times over in legal fees saved and adverse judgments avoided.

I recommend a corporate résumé in story form, written by the entrepreneur in his own words and including all aspects, good and bad, of the business. The industry, the niche, competitors, corporate strengths and weaknesses, opportunities, danger signals, a frank appraisal of key employees, banking relationships, and so on. Too much is always better than too little.

### Find the Right Lawyer

Here we go again. But if ever you need a good one, this is the time. A competent lawyer (yours should be better than theirs because of the likelihood that the two of them will meet again) is a must to represent your interests in the drafting of both the letter of intent and the subsequent purchase agreement. Yours and theirs will be meeting and competing face-to-face and brain-to-brain many times as the sales process unfolds, as well as in any after-the-sale litigation or arbitration.

Once again, your future is in the hands of the legal profession.

Be sure that the attorney you select has experience on both the acquisition and the sales sides of the process. And plenty of both if the deal is complex. No rookies allowed when your future is at stake. Ask for a list of the lawyer's past acquisitional clients, and check references carefully.

### Find a Business Broker

Like their counterparts in real estate and securities, there are more than enough business brokers to go around. Your accountants and lawyers will have a lengthy list of qualified candidates to choose from. Business brokers come in all sizes and qualities, and the rules by which they operate are vague. Watch out—their industry is largely unregulated. Just about anything goes.

Check references closely. Look at several brokers before making a decision. Remember, they want the listing, and in order to get it the unscrupulous among them will not be above outlining a scenario that may be impossible to deliver. As you would with politicians, beware of brokers making gilded promises.

Be honest with your broker; reveal early on in the discussions your company's weaknesses as well as its strengths. Eventually the broker and the prospective buyer must uncover the truth. Better sooner, while your credibility is still intact, than later.

Broker fees run anywhere from 2 percent to 12 percent dependent upon the size of the deal. Most good brokers will ask for a downstroke to cover the eventuality of seller's remorse.

Good brokers are worth every penny they are paid if they can lead us to the right buyer and help us make the deal that works. And sticks.

### Determine the Parameters of a Selling Price

As a general rule, the determination of the sales price is accomplished by the use of a price/earnings multiplier. This multiplier is a number representing a perception of the company's future earning capability. For instance, if the agreed-upon multiplier is five, the selling price would be determined by multiplying prior-year corporate earnings by five. The higher the multiple, the higher the perceived prospects for future earnings. The lower the multiple, the lower the perceived prospects.

Multiples on New York Stock Exchange listed companies range anywhere from one to infinity (when there are no earnings), with the majority falling somewhere between six and twenty. The multiple for a typical small business sale is usually somewhere between three and eight.

For the company with little or no earnings but worthwhile prospects, the selling price might be based on a multiple of assets, or on a negotiated figure that represents the buyer's perception of the opportunity the acquired company offers. Instinct and anticipation are the two ingredients in this computation. Formulas don't apply here.

Your business broker can advise you at the outset whether or not the price you expect is doable. Scrupulous and good brokers will usually back off if they determine up front your expectations are too high. They have better things to do than pursue a sale where the demands are unattainable.

Be aware that most entrepreneurs' initial expectations of what their company is worth are nonsensical. Make sure your broker and you agree on basic pricing parameters before you begin.


**Notify the Employees**

OK, I know there are sellers who attempt to peddle their companies without notifying the employees until after the deal is done.

Not only is that wrong, it seldom works.

Employees have a right to know their company is for sale. It is their lives that are being upended as well as yours. Most employees will adopt a wait-and-see attitude toward incoming management. Few, if any, will make the choice to leave until they have had a good look at the new owners. (Who knows, despite your logical, enlightened, and sparkling leadership, new management might be an improvement.)

Once you've made the decision to put the company on the market, it won't be long until there is a throng of unfamiliar faces in an information-gathering frenzy cluttering up the office. Your employees will draw their own conclusions about the crowd and will not appreciate being uninformed. It is best you let them know up front.

## Letter of Intent

When a financially qualified buyer has been located (your business broker knows how to qualify buyers) and the buyer and seller have determined that their needs are compatible, you will need a letter of intent. This document is an interim agreement between buyer and seller suspending negotiations with other potential buyers and setting the stage for a to-be-designated period of extensive due diligence. The letter of intent should be prepared by both sides' attorneys and should include signing deadlines (for both the letter of intent and the purchase agreement), escape clauses based on due diligence findings, payment terms, confidentiality, exclusivity for the buyer, and a determination of what is to be sold—assets or stock.

Once the letter of intent is prepared and signed, let the due diligence begin.

## Due Diligence

Due diligence is an integral part of the selling process. If you want the sale to progress in a spirit of goodwill, you must assist the buyer in completing his fact-finding efforts, no matter how painful the process. The more thorough his due diligence, the less chance there will be for further litigation.

Employees must be made aware of the intention to sell by this time, if the buyer is to effectively complete his due diligence. His accountants are about to descend upon your files and he is about to interview your key employees, vendors, and customers. Your business is going to be disrupted, dissected, investigated, and bared to the bone, if the buyer performs his due diligence to the depths that he should.

The valuation of inventory is often the fuzziest question in the due diligence process. It is also the most cumbersome barrier to mutual agreement on price, and the primary cause of future litigation or arbitration. Make sure that your inventory is in good order before the buyer's accountants move in to account for and appraise it. Be prepared to justify its age as well as your assigned unit costs.

And, lest you have forgotten, due diligence is not the duty solely of the buyer, a point I will discuss further in the following chapter.

The importance of due diligence is not to be taken lightly. Don't skimp on yours. A good buyer shouldn't cut corners on his. While the process itself may be aggravating and mired in details, remember that a buyer whose due diligence is sloppy will probably manage your business in a similar fashion. Do you care? Damn right you do, if you are carrying his paper, continuing in the business yourself, or have compassion for those employees who will remain.

### The Purchase Agreement

The purchase agreement requires a chapter of its own. See chapter 46.

### The Transition to New Ownership

The degree of the entrepreneur's participation in the new owner's management will depend on the buyer's wishes. The options include a wide range of choices, ranging from immediate and thorough exclusion (when the buyer wants to effect an immediate top-to-bottom change in culture), to retaining the seller in a full-time position over a specified period of time.

Beware of accepting lengthy management contracts. The ability to take direction from others has never been one of an entrepreneur's strengths.

### THE BOTTOM LINE

There is a defined and well-oiled process to follow once the commitment is made to sell the company. It is important that each step take place in the proper order.

The buyer should be allowed as much access to the company's records and to its employees as he wishes.

Share the bad news as well as the good with the buyer. After-the-sale bad news is only good news for the lawyers.

The two most important outside players on the selling team are the business broker and the attorney. The broker will help you collect your money, the lawyer will help you keep it.

# 45

## DUE DILIGENCE

LET THE BUYER beware, the old saying goes. Well, maybe that's true when we're buying a used car, but not when our company is on the line. More to the point, let the seller beware, as he prepares to exchange his life's work for a handful of cash and a promise to pay.

I must warn you, due diligence is not for buyers alone.

Suppose you've made the commitment to sell. You've asked the hard questions, searched your soul, eyed your future, and subdued your seller's remorse. Your employees have been notified, and your broker is out knocking on doors.

Along comes Mr. Big Guy. Business titan. Pillar of the community. Cash fluttering from every pocket. He informs you that you have exactly the company he has been looking for. What a coincidence, you reply, he has exactly the cash you have been looking for. A marriage made in heaven, you think, as liquidity taints your every thought. You sign a letter of intent as Big Guy looks on with a smile.

Then Big Guy gets serious. He sends in his legions of burrowing accountants. They bury their eyeshades in your filing cabinets, scrutinizing everything from tax returns to cash-flow statements, inventory values to Coke machine receipts. If Big Guy's bean counters do their job, and they damn well better, it won't be long until he knows more about your company than you do.

And auditing isn't the only thing Big Guy is doing. Here is a partial list of additional due diligence projects any Big Guy worth his suspenders will undertake:

**1.** Legal searches on you and your company. Liens, litigations, tax problems, court records, any brushes you might have had with federal and state agencies, nothing will escape his practiced eye. (Nor should it.)

**2.** Personal background searches on you and your key employees.

**3.** Research of the industry to determine its viability and its future.

**4.** Interviews with a sampling of outsiders connected with your company, including customers, bankers, vendors, and yes, even competitors.

**5.** Interviews with your key employees—without you in attendance—to glean inside information that even you don't know. At the same time that Big Guy is evaluating your company he is appraising your people, determining who will stay and who will go.

**6.** And finally, Big Guy will strap on the brightest, softest, warmest smile he owns, as he passes out his compliments on the fine company you have created. And there it will remain until D day has passed.

Meanwhile, amid this avalanche of due diligence by the party of the second part, what will you, the party of the first part, be doing? You'll be 1) making a few phone calls to inquire of Big Guy's golf handicap and 2) purchasing a new set of clubs.

What's wrong with this picture?

Assuming that Big Guy wants you to carry his paper, which every Big Guy worth his weight in subordinated notes does, you are about to become a long-term, no-voice creditor of his. Your financial future is about to rest in his hands. Big Guy, a fellow you didn't know two months ago and might not care to know today, if he didn't have something you want. Big Guy, a tough combatant and a weathered survivor in a rough-and-tumble arena where the head damn well better take precedence over the heart.

And yet, he does 95 percent of the due diligence, and you do 5 percent.

And then your company must succeed and even prosper under this man's management. If it doesn't, instead of a ticket to Palm Springs, you've got a ticket to the courthouse.

Here is the due diligence you should have been doing at the same time Big Guy was churning his way through your past:

**1.** What does he want from your company? Are his goals similar to yours? It's OK if they aren't, but will your key employees be able to swallow his revised versions? Which of your current employees are key to his success? Will they remain? Who will depart? Can the new company survive if they leave?

**2.** Does Big Guy bring something to your company's table that was not there before? (Besides cash, which by itself is never enough.) Management expertise? Access to new markets? New distribution? If cash is his only additional baggage, how does he expect to maintain, let alone expand, your business?

**3.** Is Big Guy's management style similar to yours? Do those who have worked for him speak well of him as a manager? A leader? A human being? Does he manage by intimidation, flaunt his power, spend money lavishly, terminate employees indiscriminately? Will your employees be able to adapt to his management style?

It is acceptable (often preferable) for the new management style to differ from yours, but you must go into the sale with a well-grounded idea of the changes your employees will face.

**4.** Is Big Guy's personal life in sync with his managerial image? Are you comfortable entrusting 75 percent of your life savings to this person? Are you comfortable entrusting the careers and the futures of your employees and friends to him?

**5.** Is Big Guy's previous business experience transferable to your company? Does he have industry experience? Is his experience in products or in services? Small business or big business.?

**6.** Are Big Guy's ethics similar to yours? If they aren't, there's sure to be trouble on the horizon. Ethics, his or yours, aren't going to change as a result of a business deal.

The typical small business sale includes a cash downstroke (25 percent or so) with the majority in paper (usually a note, subordinated to bank debt) spread over too many years. An entirely new form of risk has now evolved for you, the difference being that you no longer have a voice in the decisions that will govern your financial future.

*You are turning over three-quarters of your life savings to a stranger—some guy off the street!*

He'd better be good.

Lopsided due diligence comes from your impatience to get the deal done.

The downside, one last time, has been overlooked.

## THE BOTTOM LINE

Due diligence goes in both directions. Be as interested in the buyer's history as he is in yours.

The buyer's past will foretell his future. The more due diligence you perform, the more you will learn of his past, and the better you can predict his future. And yours.

Unless it's a straight cash deal, you cannot walk away after the sale. Do whatever it takes to assure that the business continues to prosper after you've gone.

And finally, if trust is an issue, don't do the deal, no matter how good the downstroke looks.

# 46

# THE PURCHASE
# AGREEMENT

HIRE THE BEST damn lawyer in town to draft the purchase agreement. Hell, hire the two best lawyers in town. Hire a firm, an army, an endless horde.

But it won't make a whit of difference, because there isn't any such thing as an ironclad purchase agreement. If the party of the second part decides to violate it, then by God, it is about to be violated. Forget what it says or how well it says it.

The good news is that justice usually will be served. The legal system, as cumbersome and flawed as it is, will see to that—if you can afford to feed its meter. The bad news is that justice can take three years to arrive, which will seem like a lifetime under the stress of litigation. The further bad news is that it will cost you an arm and a leg in legal fees to uphold what the purchase agreement couldn't.

In order to avoid a mountain of legal fees at the back end of the purchase agreement, it is necessary to dispense a lesser, but still ample, amount at the front end. Or stated another way, the better the lawyer the more obvious any violation of the purchase agreement will be. And the more obvious the violation, the more readily the party of the second part will ultimately be nailed when he decides to disregard it or violate it.

Here are some suggestions on the subject of purchase agreements:

**1.** Absolutely, positively insist on, demand, clamor for, and stipulate that the purchase agreement call for arbitration, not litigation, to settle any disputes. Arbitration is one-half as expensive and takes one-half of the time. (One year versus two or more.)

Secondary bonus: Arbitration doesn't allow for appeals.

**2.** The issue will arise, if it hasn't already, of whether assets or stock is being sold. This determination will ultimately be negotiated and has benefits to both parties, because of the tax liability implications. In short, it is to the seller's advantage to sell stock, the buyer's to buy assets. The advantages to the two parties are not compatible, and either the buyer or the seller must make a negotiated concession. Make sure that if you make it, you are compensated somewhere else. Your tax accountant can advise you as to the costs associated with the trade-off.

**3.** The seller's natural tendency during the course of negotiations is to pay most of his attention to the moneyed issues. Price, payment terms, reserve baskets, and so on. Meanwhile, the party of the second part is noisily granting those short-sighted, dollar-speckled requests while quietly taking those not-so-obvious trade-offs that open the door for him to beat your brains out a year or two later when the company isn't performing up to his expectations.

**4.** Pay the closest attention to the breach-of-contract covenants, particularly those specifying the withholding of payments. This is the first page the buyer and his lawyer will turn to after determining that you have violated the ironclad purchase agreement.

**5.** Whatever you do, insist that any withheld payments be put into escrow.

All of which is not to say that the terms governing the withholding of payments can, or should, be made to protect only the seller. They can't. And shouldn't. The party of the second part needs protection too. Big Guys are not always wrong and Little Guys are not always right.

**6.** Assume the absolute worst when drawing up the purchase agreement (the downside issue again). Assume that Big Guy will be at your throat a year from now. And you at his. (Statistics support this assumption.)

Then cross your fingers, do what you can to help, and pray that Big Guy is as adept at managing businesses as he is at buying them.

## THE BOTTOM LINE

In the long term, a well-written purchase agreement will protect the seller's interests. In the short term, it won't.

The only short-term protection against a buyer's violation of the purchase agreement is his ethics and the degree of his success in running the business.

And, lest you've forgotten, your eyes were open when you jumped into bed with him.

# 47

---

## THE UNWRITTEN
## RULE OF CASH

---

ONCE UPON A time there was a sweat-stained entrepreneur. This entrepreneur was known to his customers as Leonard Littleguy, and he produced the finest ratchets in the land. The Littleguy Ratchet Company provided jobs for four hundred employees and was so successful that lush, green plants adorned his reception area while voice-mail systems sat on every desk.

But Littleguy was unhappy. He spent his days managing problems, facing conflicts, and motivating people, while his entrepreneurial talents fizzled and disappeared. Apathy was his constant companion.

Whereupon he decided to sell his company.

A host of prospective buyers descended upon him like lawyers surrounding a freeway pileup. Bartholomew Bigguy, a pillar within the community, quickly rose above the pack. (Bigguy had always lusted for a foothold in the ratchet industry, although he himself was unable to tell the difference between a ratchet and a thingamabob.)

Whereupon Bigguy offered Littleguy X dollars for his company. Littleguy replied, "No thanks," pointing out that the correct value was X plus X, whereupon Bigguy smiled broadly and agreed. The two men exchanged warm handshakes and kind words, as Littleguy marveled at his negotiating prowess.

Littleguy soon possessed an expensive ironclad purchase agreement for X plus X, along with a small sack of cash and a subordinated note that would begin making principal payments sometime in the twilight zone. Happily clutching his sack of cash and reveling in his freedom from debt, he shuttled off to Palm Springs where he purchased a very fine set of golf clubs.

One year passed. Rather than the giant bank draft Littleguy expected as his first annual interest payment, he was greeted by a giant claim, citing his breach of contract. Bigguy, the giant claim informed him, expected giant indemnification from Littleguy as a result of giant overstatements of assets, giant understatements of liabilities, and a leaky faucet in the men's room.

Littleguy phoned his lawyer.

"Call the cops," he screamed, wiping sweat from his brow. "Bigguy's got my dough."

"The cops can't help," his attorney replied.

"But I haven't been proved guilty and Bigguy kept my dough."

"Doesn't matter. The rule of cash takes precedence."

"The rule of cash?" Littleguy choked. "What's that?"

"Whosoever controlleth the checkbook maketh the rules," the attorney replied, brushing a speck of dust from his shoe.

"But what about my ironclad purchase agreement?" Littleguy wailed.

"Sorry. The rule of cash takes precedence."

"So what do I do now?" moaned Littleguy, visions of legal meters spinning in his head.

"If this goes according to the usual breach and indemnify M.O., it should reach the courts in about two years," the attorney replied. "But not to worry, the two of you will settle before it comes to trial."

"We will?" Littleguy gasped, astounded that his lawyer was so clairvoyant. "What will we settle for?"

"X."

"X? But that was Bigguy's original offer," Littleguy sputtered.

"Yep," the attorney replied, adjusting his suspenders.

"And I'll be back where I started?"

"Not quite. Don't forget my legal fees."

"How much?" Littleguy whispered, holding his head in his hands.

"Not much. Maybe one-half of X."

And so it was that Leonard Littleguy became educated in the manner in which small companies are acquired. It was soon thereafter that Leonard traded in his golf clubs for two aprons, and he and Mrs. Littleguy can today be found spooning frozen yogurt in the desert paradise of Palm Springs.

Meanwhile, Bigguy sold the Littleguy Ratchet Company for X plus X to a major ratchet manufacturer.

## THE BOTTOM LINE

Get cash.

Do as much due diligence on Bigguy as he does on you.

Get cash.

Find a motivated lawyer who has previous experience with the acquisition professionals. Then listen.

And get cash.

# 48

## AFTER
## THE SALE

THE GOOD NEWS is we're off the hook. We don't owe our vendors and bankers seven figures any more.

The bad news is it isn't as easy as we thought it would be, standing idly on the sidelines, watching our company underachieve.

National Screenprint was purchased by two Minneapolis businessmen, one an accountant, the other a banker. Neither were small businessmen, and neither had experience in the imprinted sportswear industry. Nevertheless, three months after the sale was finalized, National Screenprint had a new CEO, president, sales manager, CFO, and director of purchasing. All rookies to the industry.

Approximately the same day that the last of the old guard departed, the busy season arrived. With a vengeance, as is typical for those who have chosen to make their living on the coattails of the national retailers.

You guessed it. My phone started to ring. And ring. Old employees were irate. And confused. And disheartened. This decision was wrong, and that decision made no sense, and the company was going straight to hell, and what was I going to do? Their complaints were endless, their indictments harsh. I was caught in the middle.

I did the only thing I could. I relayed their complaints to the new owners, swallowed my tongue, and supported their decisions.

The number one ex-owner rule, whether he is retained or put out to pasture, is to be supportive of the new owners, whether they deserve it or not. Your best interests can only be served if the new company wins. Inciting the troops and taking potshots at management will only decrease any chances you have of collecting long-deferred payouts, and strengthen the chances of after-the-sale litigation.

It won't be easy, as this subdued reaction runs counter to your entrepreneurial grain. It's damn tough to sit on the sidelines, supporting decisions that twenty years of experience say are wrong. But the entrepreneur's support is an essential element in the successful acquisitional process.

The number two ex-owner rule is to blend in with the landscape. There is a culture change going on within your old company, and you are no longer in the culture-establishing business. The new owners have purchased the right to insert a culture of their own.

So smile, nod dumbly, and shut up. The buyers—hopefully—will institute the new culture gradually, if they have done their homework on the process of postacquisitional management. Besides, the old culture was not exactly the Little House on the Prairie. The company needed something fresh and new.

The downside of excessive and/or disruptive entrepreneurial involvement? Lawsuits at best, the demise of the new ownership, along with their promise to pay, at worst.

They paid cash and assumed debt for the company and they deserve the opportunity to make changes without our second-guessing. They also deserve the time to make their changes stick. Naturally we won't agree with everything they do. So what's new?

It's amazing how any presale misrepresentations and postsale transgressions will be overlooked if the acquisition performs to the buyer's expectations.

And it's also amazing what will happen when it doesn't.

## THE BOTTOM LINE

It is in your best interests to do whatever you can to assure that the new owners are successful. You can abet their chances of success by being supportive of their policies and decisions and by remaining quietly in the background as they go about managing their company their way.

# IX

## THE ENTREPRENEUR:
## WHO WE ARE AND
## WHY WE PERSEVERE

# 49

## THE INGREDIENTS
## WE NEED TO SURVIVE

THE ODDS AGAINST entrepreneurial success are enough to keep the average working stiff on somebody else's payroll. Those lousy odds—five-to-one are the ones most often quoted—are the result of the vast number of skills necessary for entrepreneurial success. Some of those skills are trainable: financial understanding, hiring skills, organizational structure, ability to communicate, and a long list of unexciting but managerially desirable attributes.

In addition to these trainable skills, there is a continual need for help from above. Old-fashioned luck plays an important role in the development of any successful business: the chance discovery of an unpopulated niche, availability of capital, decisions of competitors, trends in the industry, the direction of the economy.

There are, however, several entrepreneurial ingredients that can be neither learned nor left to luck. They are God-given ingredients, without which the prospective entrepreneur might just as well pursue the cursed paycheck. We either have them or we don't. They include:

- Intuition
- Living with risk and debt

- Eternal optimism
- The Urge

## Intuition

OK, so everybody has intuition. Your barber already knows the winner of this weekend's Notre Dame game, your son knows Bart Simpson's impending fate, your golf partner knows he owns the next hole.

But barbers, sons, and golf partners are probably wrong 50 percent of the time. After all, intuition doesn't have to be right to be intuition.

Unless your business depends upon it.

Imagine it's decision time at General Motors. The powers-that-be summon the lawyers, the consultants, the army of specialists. They huddle, review, and compute. After an eternity of conferring, the pinstriped troops reach consensus, never forgetting there is security in numbers (in the event their decision should raise the CEO's eyebrows).

The scene shifts now to decision time at your company. There's no time for meetings, and nobody to meet with anyway. Hopefully the homework is done and you've asked the right questions. You close the door, take the phone off the hook, scratch your chin, and stare out the window. Wham—the answer arrives from nowhere, like a Muhammad Ali left jab.

Call it intuition, or call it gut instinct, or call it rolling the dice. But you had better call it right more often than wrong, or you'll soon be calling it quits.

Accurate decision making by the entrepreneur can be aided and abetted by a lofty IQ. Advanced education and training can't hurt, either. But it doesn't take an M.B.A. or a Ph.D. to get to know your customer, your product, and your niche better than anybody else.

The General Motors gang had better be right 75 percent of the time or they won't be invited to the next meeting. The entrepreneur had better be right 75 percent of the time or he *will* be invited to the next meeting—with a banker, a lawyer, and a judge.

I'm not advocating that intuition should replace planning, listening, and employee participation in the decision-making process. The successful entrepreneurs learn that all are necessary, more so as the company expands.

But somebody must make the final decision. Somebody must break the ties. That somebody is you.

In the end, trust your gut.

It got you this far.


## Living with Risk and Debt

It's September of 1989, and my company is in the midst of another frantic back-to-school season. Our retail customers scream—not timidly, mind you—for more product. *Now!* Our employees work around the clock to keep customer expectations and delivery somewhat in balance.

Meanwhile, our revolving credit line breaks the $6 million barrier as receivables, inventory, and work-in-process soar. Every penny of that $6 million is, gulp, guaranteed by me.

And that's not all. Tack on another $1.5 million or so that our vendors expect within 30 days. Again guaranteed by me.

Which now makes $7.5 million floating around town that I have guaranteed. Not bad for a guy whose net worth is one-tenth of that. I lie in bed in the early-morning hours praying that my creditors don't all come knocking at the same time, and my debtors don't all take Chapter 11.

And so goes another day in the life of the entrepreneur, under a cloud of never-ending debt: debt that doesn't go on vacation, debt that knows no holidays. Debt that ticks while you sleep and hangs around over the weekends, like an unwanted houseguest.

Typically, the more sales growth you experience, the higher the tower of debt becomes. Debt-decreasing options include putting the brakes on sales growth, recording a degree of profitability that outpaces sales growth, selling the business, or going public.

Undaunted by this specter of never-ending debt, I continued for twenty years to guarantee more and more of it. Meanwhile, the marketplace does not return the favor—it guarantees nothing. To the contrary, interest rates soar, competitors attack, and old niches disappear. Still the cloud of debt hovers menacingly overhead, always out of reach and always larger than before.

The entrepreneur must have an inbred indifference (built on brimming self-confidence) to the consequences of signing his name to a guarantee. As reliable as snow during a Minnesota December, the personal guarantee comes with the entrepreneurial turf.

While risk taking and the accumulation of debt are necessary to the business of doing business, the element of risk taking inherent in entrepreneuring is not to be confused with gambling. Gambling means you play *their* game. Risk taking means you play *your* game. Gambling means you can't change the odds by perseverance and hard work. Risk taking means you can. In gambling, you either win or you lose. Risk taking encompasses points between.

Frankly, gambling scares the hell out of me. I get queasy while waiting for the dealer's next card at a Las Vegas $2 blackjack table. The cowboy next to me, in tattered jeans and aging Stetson, yawns and makes a six-pack disappear, as he plays each game for a considerable percentage of his net worth. Breathing hard and awash in perspiration, I drop $34.

Back home, my $6 million debt bomb ticks on, never missing a beat.

### Eternal Optimism

Successful entrepreneurs view the world through rose-tinted sunglasses. Rarely pessimistic, they see:

- Opportunities, not problems
- Good fortune, not misfortune
- Trust, not mistrust
- Upsides, not downsides

If these downsides were given a priority in strategic decisions, the entrepreneur would be a threatened species. He might be a lawyer instead, or work for General Motors or the government.

The Macintosh would belong to IBM, and Burger King would rule the hamburger world. There are too many valid and logical reasons not to pursue that new niche, hire that new employee, open a Chicago office.

Mountains get climbed, kingdoms built, and dreams fulfilled by people who believe mountains, kingdoms, and dreams are attainable. Sir Edmund Hillary stole a page of history by climbing a mountain previously considered unconquerable, but not before he had convinced himself he could succeed. Would-be entrepreneurs embark on similar ascents a million times a year.

To be a successful entrepreneur, you must exude confidence and optimism in the face of those lousy odds. Like Jack Nicklaus over a curling eight-footer, Michael Jordan at the line, or Joe Montana in the pocket, you know what has to be done and are confident you're the best person for the job. Competitors who lack your unswerving confidence and pay an inordinate amount of time and attention to the possibility of losing are bound to do just that.

Entrepreneurial optimism must come in a degree that doesn't damage vision. I am not advocating downside blindness as a business strategy. Your company most certainly needs a designated rein puller to worry about the downsides, but that person is usually not going to be you.

The financial person is normally the designated rein puller, at least during the evolutionary stage of growth. He's bred for the job, or at least the good ones are. In later years the naysayer role can be delegated to a professional manager, brought in to explore and prepare for downsides, among other things. Professional managers and financial people improve and build, but rarely do they create. Everybody has a role.

I made it through four successful start-ups and twenty-two years of knee-knocking entrepreneurship before my unchecked optimism got me in trouble. Two nice-guy CFOs, both as optimistic as I, joined me in neglecting the blips that came marching across our business screen.

In retrospect, I should have learned to curtail my too-rosy optimism. Like most entrepreneurs, however, I have this inbred need to see something positive in a rainy day, a grouchy employee, or another Minnesota Viking Super Bowl loss. I enjoy viewing the world through my rose-tinted sunglasses and feel sorry for those who don't.

I'd rather hire a devil's advocate than become one myself.

## The Urge

I remember the first time I felt The Urge. I was twelve or so when my dad brought home our first family dog. Christened Jack, he was one of those pint-sized yippers that Zsa Zsa Gabor might own, with the same nervous disposition. Jack didn't really fit our family; I think my dad got railroaded. We both would have preferred something with a deeper bark.

We lived two blocks from the Waveland Golf Course, a hilly, wooded provider of joy in the western part of Des Moines. Soon after Jack's arrival, I discovered his role in my life. His nose could sniff out golf balls. Lost golf balls.

Jack would disappear into the woods, soon to return with golf ball and wagging tail. After a hasty dog snack (positive reinforcement, in managerial jargon), back to the boondocks he'd go. So efficient was that nose that on several occasions he exhumed those ancient balls with the diamond-patterned covers that even my father could barely recall.

Thanks to Jack, I was the king of the golf-course groupies those two summers. I played with new balls, the envy of my peers. More important, my market share of Waveland's used golf ball sales went from 10 percent to 90 percent, as a result of the reliable influx of inventory. I cleared over $500 during those two summers (after dog-bone expenses), a tidy sum for a kid in those days.

My first entrepreneurial venture. Assets were one small dog. Zero receivables, no annual performance reviews, no OSHA, no bankers, bare-bones inventory. Negligible investment, minimal risk. An entrepreneur's dream.

Those two summers marked the birth of The Urge for me. I tried several other kid businesses over the succeeding years, and ultimately selected my career, or let it select me, based on the success of my early partnership with Jack.

The Urge. Like the craving for popcorn or chocolate-covered turtles. It never goes away.

## THE BOTTOM LINE

**Intuition:** You live or you die on the accuracy of your intuition. You had better be right 75 percent of the time.

**Risk and debt:** Be able to, or learn to, live under a cloud of risk and debt. Always a part of building a business, they will be there until the day the company is sold.

**Eternal optimism:** An entrepreneur must be the eternal optimist. That optimism needs to be controlled, however, either by making the necessary personal adjustment or by hiring an in-house devil's advocate.

**The Urge:** Every successful entrepreneur harbors The Urge. The Urge usually surfaces at an early age, and even the smallest of successes can fuel its growth.

# 50

---

# THE STEREOTYPICAL
# ENTREPRENEUR

---

EVERY PROFESSION HAS its stereotypes. If I say "lawyer," most of us can rattle off a half dozen lawyerly traits without pausing for breath. Ditto politicians, accountants, and athletes. We all get typecast, sooner or later.

Well, entrepreneurs are people too. We have tendencies and preferences and traits, like everybody else. A glimpse of these can give the nonentrepreneur an insight into how to deal with us. For instance:

1. You are a lawyer and want to become an entrepreneur's best friend. Forget it.
2. You are an entrepreneur's spouse and want to have a lavish cocktail party to celebrate a birthday. Don't.
3. You are an entrepreneur's employee and have this crazy idea about selling snowmobiles in the Virgin Islands. Tell him.
4. You are looking for a job with an entrepreneur's company, but don't want to work on Saturdays. Keep on looking.

There is something here for everyone:

ENTREPRENEURIAL LIKES

New ideas

Niches

Creative people

Accountants

Customers

Activity/motion

Perspiration

A good crisis

Falling interest rates

Time alone

Early-morning hours

Saturdays

Winning at anything

ENTREPRENEURIAL DISLIKES

Meetings

Details

Paperwork

Coats and ties

Marketing strategies, position papers, five-year plans, job descriptions, etc.

Rules

Most bankers

Most consultants

All lawyers

All governmental agencies

Authority

Rising interest rates

Parties, especially cocktail

Schmoozing

Employees who leave at 5:00

## THE BOTTOM LINE

A glimpse at the stereotypical entrepreneur reveals why they are the designated risk takers, innovators, and loners of the business world.

The same glimpse reveals why they reinvent the business wheel every day and why their attempts to become organized, focused, and managerial are such a monumental struggle.

# 51

## THE ULTIMATE
## UPSIDE

SEVERAL YEARS AGO, I listened to a fellow from R. J. Reynolds's Chicago office tell me his version of corporate life on the fast track. We were wilting side by side in a Jacuzzi somewhere in Southern California—my idyllic vacation, his average business meeting. He talked of his place under Reynolds's corporate sun as we tried to forget another midwestern winter.

His lament? Over 50 percent of his working time was spent dealing with political matters within his workday environment—not performing his defined duties, which happened to be marketing. The success or failure of his career, he went on, depended on an individual or committee "up there somewhere." And those individuals or committees up there somewhere always seemed to need oiling or greasing, coddling or soothing. Job performance at R. J. Reynolds, he felt, was secondary to the conduct of politics.

My friend's tales of corporate woe included schmoozing, positioning, and a wide variety of other nonproductive activities. All a part of the corporate politicking process, I assume, but not a part of Reynolds's corporate mission. Or so I'd bet, anyway.

Our discussion that day served to reaffirm old knowledge. The grass was still greener on my side of the fence.

I'm the first to admit my company was not free of its own cultural and political idiosyncrasies. If it had been, I would still be there, at work, and not here, hunched over my PC. We had plenty of quirks of our own that weren't conducive to accomplishing our corporate objectives. Unlike the Reynolds guy, however, I—yes I—had the ability to change what my company believed and the manner in which we performed. I didn't have to hang around the water cooler, complaining about somebody upstairs. I *was* that somebody upstairs.

In short, my Jacuzzi friend did not have the option to effect a change in his culture. He had to live or die within his work environment. His only two options were to love it or leave it.

The ultimate entrepreneurial upside is not fame, fortune, accolades or, in my case, all the imprinted sportswear I could take home. (These dividends are not to be discounted, however.) The ultimate upside is the control we have over our own destiny.

We alone have the opportunity to establish, maintain, and change our business environment and our corporate culture. We alone control our company's view of products, customers, and employees—the key to any marketplace.

Thus it is the marketplace that ultimately determines our fate: through the medium of our customers and our employees and the way we choose to brew the lot of them together. If we enhance the fate of our customers, we survive and prosper. If we don't, we get what we deserve. That's nature's way.

Sure, there's a handful of unfriendly land mines along the path to the marketplace. These include interest rates, the government, competitors, quirky bankers, and the economy, to name a few.

But if we manage our business logically, these random and sometimes malicious events should result in blips and not trends. The marketplace will prevail. It always has.

I want my success to be dependent upon my ability to satisfy customers' needs. I want the marketplace to determine my fate, not the midwestern regional manager. I want to spend my time searching for new customers, taking care of old ones, and producing quality products. I don't want to spend my time schmoozing, positioning, or covering my ass.

Business is tough enough the way it is.

## THE BOTTOM LINE

Of all the upsides of an entrepreneurial career (and there are many), the most meaningful is the ability to establish, maintain, and alter your own destiny.

The good news is that no one but the marketplace can judge your performance.

The bad news is there is no one to blame but yourself when things go wrong.

# 52

## THE ULTIMATE DOWNSIDE

THE GAME-ENDING whistle mercifully ends another Super Bowl blowout. The crestfallen losers limp back to the locker room to commiserate with their teammates over what might have been. Hometown fans grieve for their fallen warriors, who have given so much over the season and now must suffer the bitterness of defeat. Seven months of hard play shot to hell.

Well, almost shot to hell. The following day it's off to the bank as our now-recovered losers deposit the losers' spoils. To be followed by five months of recuperation on faraway beaches, interrupted only by the emotional strain of renegotiating their fairyland contracts.

That's losing?

Try Chapter 7 for unadulterated losing. First you lose the team. Then it's adios to the coaches, players, trainers, and ball boys. You lose the showers, the football field, and the uniforms. Next goes your desk, your job, and your life savings. Your kid's education. Your hope. Your future.

That's losing!

The deposed Fortune 500 executive reluctantly bids farewell to his bereaved corporate mates amid a flurry of last-minute handouts. Severance packages, golden parachutes, and job placement assistance lead the list of gifts bestowed on the departing executive. Meanwhile, his stock in the company continues to trade publicly and have ongoing value, should he need instant cash to pay his golf club dues.

That's losing?

The failed entrepreneur retains his wife, the kids, the house, and his lousy credit rating while creditors walk off with the rest. He receives no severance pay. There is no golden parachute as he leaves his life behind.

He owns no stock. There is no company.

That's losing!

The displaced executive finds a displaced-executive head-hunter. If times are really tough, he accepts a lesser position, and may even take a 10 percent salary cut. In the worst case, he pays his own country club dues and drives his own Cadillac.

That's losing?

Our previously failed entrepreneur, armed with a new vision, hits the funding circuit. A chorus of hearty nos greets his beleaguered ears, followed by a succession of revolving doors. "Once a loser, always a loser" is the conventional wisdom in the world of today's debt-and-equity providers.

To the want ads he turns (no headhunters specialize in failed entrepreneurs), finally hungry enough to exchange servitude for wages. He finds nothing under "Bosses." No positions available for "Ex-entrepreneurs." Grasping at straws now, he tries "Situations Wanted," then "Between Opportunities," and finally "Down on the Luck."

Still nothing.

Jobs are for the rest of the world. There is no published demand for entrepreneurs, failed or otherwise.

You either create your own demand, or you starve.

## THE BOTTOM LINE

As an entrepreneur, you risk it all, from your personal assets to your future. There is no recourse to Chapter 7. Opportunities for reemergence following failures are rare.

Nothing compares to this degree of risk taking in any other segment of the business world.

# 53

## ENTREPRENEURIAL
## TERROR

NO PAIN, NO gain, the old saying goes. Coined, no doubt, by another undercapitalized entrepreneur greeting a spouse over breakfast, after another sleepless night. Sleeplessness brought on by entrepreneurial terror, that dependable midnight visitor.

Entrepreneurial terror. Worry, loneliness, and desperation, in its most advanced stage. As real as unemployment compensation and as dependable as a computer breakdown. As much a part of owning a business as sixty-hour workweeks, customers who don't pay their bills, and employees who don't show up for work.

Entrepreneurial terror evolves from a wide variety of sources: the shadowy phone conversation with the banker who wants to discuss the loan committee's response to the latest disappointing financial statements; rumors of the impending defection of our number one salesperson; yesterday's guarded phone call from our best customer asking to meet with us tomorrow.

So why is entrepreneurial terror any worse than the slings and arrows that assault the rest of the world? After all, rain falls on everyone's parade.

Because entrepreneurial terror, similar to the vocation it haunts, is a solo voyage. Lindbergh to Paris. No one else can share the risk, comprehend the danger, or imagine the consequences. Only we understand the spectrum of our choices and the pain of our punishments. We are the president with the veto power. The governor who can stay the execution.

We stand to lose it all, a situation outsiders can never understand. Everything we've worked for is vulnerable—our dreams, our pride, our ego. We stand to lose our belongings, personal as well as business. And we stand to hurt our shareholders, our employees, and our family, as well as ourselves.

Entrepreneurial terror is usually preceded by entrepreneurial worry. Worry is natural and, in its moderate stages, can be constructive and even help resolve issues. The surviving entrepreneur recognizes that worry is a necessary stage of the problem-solving process. But when left unchecked, worry turns into terror, which neither is healthy nor resolves anything.

The effects of entrepreneurial terror can be minimized by persistence, hard work, and commitment. A dose of luck is always welcome as well. But, like football knees and tennis elbows, terror is one of the prices that must be paid to play the entrepreneurial game.

## THE BOTTOM LINE

Entrepreneurial terror is an unwelcome part of the business-building process. It cannot be avoided, it cannot be shared, but it can be minimized by hard work and the application of sound business skills.

Worry is healthy and serves to resolve problems; terror is unhealthy and tends to either create new problems or magnify old ones.

# 54

## WHY WE ENDURE

MOST OF US do not set out with the romantic intention of creating a company on the seventh day. Who would, after all, make a rational decision to go through life without knowing the security of a paycheck? Rather, the entrepreneurial majority of us stumble upon some random business opportunity at an unpredictable point in our lives, resulting in our painting ourselves into a vocational corner from which there is no return.

For some of us, the choice to start a business is made because of some real or imagined financial opportunity. For others it comes from the lure of the power inherent in controlling the lives of others. Most of us, however, happen upon our chosen careers because we have previously learned that we are incapable of working for somebody else.

Let's face it, many of those traits that make us successful entrepreneurs work against us in the world of time clocks and paychecks. Our independence and the depths of our beliefs often make us undesirable, unhappy, and underachieving employees. I proved this myself, more than once.

Once screwed into the entrepreneurial vise, intentionally or otherwise, what is it that keeps us there? Why do we choose to endure the attendant lack of security, the never-ending financial pressure, and the emotional strains that go with assuming the responsibility of controlling the lives of others? Why do we continue to pay the price of survival—the sixty-, seventy-, and eighty-hour workweeks? Why do we resign ourselves to living in the shadow of that business we started?

It is the joy of creation and the challenge of growth.

Which is not to say there are not successful entrepreneurs among us who have placed the attainment of net worth or the wielding of power ahead of creation and growth. But creation and growth are the motivators most likely to attract worthy and committed employees.

It doesn't take long for discerning and talented employees to differentiate between the entrepreneur who is there for the money or the muscle, and the founder who wants to create and to grow. Given the two options, I ask, whose payroll would you rather be on?

Our companies develop into living, breathing organisms, existing for the world to behold, to savor or reject, born where nothing stood before. These corporate organisms create value for their customers, employees, and shareholders. They can be touched; they have a heartbeat. They are loved and, yes, sometimes hated. We are proud and, on some occasions, embarrassed.

I took a visual inventory of my company some time ago. I saw shareholder value where none had existed before, not only for me, but for a handful of deserving employees. I counted worthwhile products serving customer needs. I counted thousands of customers—satisfied customers—using our products. I counted a cadre of vendors and bankers growing in partnership with us.

And I saw a cohesive, albeit imperfect, corporate team, skilled at creating and distributing our products. That team consisted of people, two hundred of them, feeding perhaps another four hundred mouths. It was a close corporate family with caring members—a family availing itself of health plans and profit-sharing plans, offering security and opportunity to those who contribute.

It is creation, the molding of something from nothing, and growth, the feeding of that creation, that sustain our energies and drive us to persevere.

## THE BOTTOM LINE

While greed and power have been the parents of some entrepreneurial start-ups, these motives rarely beget the great companies. Where greed and power motivate the entrepreneur, they are usually turn-offs to the best employees.

Creation and growth are the true entrepreneurial parents of risk and commitment.

# X

# TIPS FOR
# SUCCESS

# 55

## MY TOP

## TWELVE TIPS

A REVIEW OF my top dozen tips, for the current or aspiring entrepreneur:

**1.** Every company has four or five game-breaking positions. The entrepreneur's number one responsibility is to assure these positions are filled with superstars.

These game-breaking positions are the CFO, along with the operations, sales, marketing, and purchasing managers. And, oh yes, you. The entrepreneur. Your number one responsibility is to hire the right people, train them, reward them, promote them, and make sure they grow as fast as or faster than your company's sales.

If they don't keep up, replace them. For their sake as well as your own.

**2.** Find a mentor—someone who has gone before. Leave trial and error to your competitors.

**3.** Nothing happens until a sale is made.

How many good products go nowhere because they don't reach the shelves?

It is sales that drive the business. Develop a sales- and customer-driven culture.

**4.** Fast, good, and cheap. Pick any two.

Serious trouble awaits those who attempt to be all things to the marketplace.

My advice? Leave the cheap to others and steer your company in the direction of fast and good.

**5.** Quality first.

The U.S. automobile industry learned this one the hard way.

If you don't have a quality program in place today, you're already far behind.

It matters little which program you choose, as long as you are committed.

**6.** All turnarounds require strategic change. Never try to grow your company out of its problems.

All companies eventually need turnarounds.

The entrepreneur's usual remedy? Throw more sales and energy at the problems.

The correct remedy? Make the required strategic changes—in yourself and your company.

Smarter, not harder.

**7.** Catch more bees with honey.

Hackneyed, but true. The "Do unto others" commandment is hard at work in today's management arena.

**8.** Things never go back to the way they were. Learn to live in today's environment.

What worked yesterday will not work tomorrow.

Change is a constant. Make responsiveness to change a company strength.

**9.** Acknowledge your mistakes.

Nobody is right all the time. It's OK for your employees to make mistakes, as long as they don't make the same one twice.

And, speaking of mistakes, you make them too. Your employees recognize them, just as you recognize theirs. Failure to acknowledge your mistakes undermines your credibility and affects your ability to lead.

Fess up.

**10.** Pick ethics.

They're due for a comeback.

**11.** Vendors are partners.

Vendors are people, too, and the good ones are as important to your future as a good customer.

Treat them as partners, not as adversaries.

**12.** Don't bite off more than you can chew.

Your resources are limited. Focus on two or three attainable objectives and complete each one before moving on.

# XI

## EPILOGUE

# 56

---

# IN DEFENSE OF
# THE ENTREPRENEUR

---

I HAVE NO problem with being put out to pasture by the professional managers who bought my company. They paid for the privilege.

I do, however, have a problem with the perception of entrepreneurs held by many professional managers, and their willingness—even eagerness—to take their educated potshots at us. Steve Bostic, CEO of R. Stevens Corp. and a PepsiCo graduate, is typical of the breed. Bostic, and others like him, seem to have an inordinate contempt for entrepreneurs and are not hesitant to let the world know of their feelings.

"Frankly," Bostic says in a December 1989 *Inc.* magazine interview, "I detest the word entrepreneur. I prefer to think of myself as an enterprising individual. Enterprising individuals are resourceful and disciplined. They've usually been educated in a corporate environment.

"In my mind," he continues, "an entrepreneur is someone who doesn't care much about information or facts. He's liable to pull out both guns at any moment and start blazing away. They're always rolling the dice."

Bostic goes on to inform us that his current business creation is being built with the unwavering purpose of selling it. "I think the worst thing you can do is to fall in love with a business and lose your objectivity. Business is a way to build equity and value."

Brrr, so detached, and oh so focused. I wonder how Bostic's loyal employees swallow his icy goals.

Sadly, most of the entrepreneurial shortcomings Bostic points out are mine. Has he been tapping my phone or opening my mail?

Fortunately for folks like me the survival and growth of our business is not based solely on such attributes as focus and order and systems and planning (although these managerial traits become increasingly important as our creations grow). Rather, our entrepreneurial growth feeds off of creativity and commitment and vision and sacrifice.

I first achieved entrepreneurship for the same reason that Harry Truman ascended to the presidency—basically, neither of us knew any better at the time. Harry and I stumbled into our jobs accidentally, with only vague ideas of what lay ahead.

In my situation I had no training, no mentoring, no business education. Basically, no nothing.

No nothing except a need to provide for my family and an overpowering urge to do it myself—my way—fostered by several previous attempts at doing it someone else's way.

As I see it, there are three paths to follow for those of us who end up owning our own businesses. Accidental, educational, and corporate.

The accidental entrepreneur (or pantser) sees a niche and tumbles into it, letting gravity take its course. He comes from nowhere and everywhere—often from a nonbusiness background—and his primary motive is, at first, sustenance, to be followed by creativity and growth.

Secondly, there is the educational entrepreneur. The focused and aspiring student (too sophisticated to be a pantser for long) gets his or her degree while learning the entrepreneurial game out of a book, digesting and ultimately regurgitating the same lessons the accidental types are learning by trial and error in an unforgiving marketplace.

And finally, there is the Bostic type, the corporate entrepreneur. The Fortune 500 bailout. Those that avail themselves of this route, enterprising individuals and professional managers alike, make their early business mistakes on someone else's time. They eventually graduate summa cum professional manager, and enter the entrepreneurial fray without ever knowing the numbing effects of trial and error management on their personal pocketbooks. Typically, their organized, systematic, managerial traits would stand in the way of begetting a start-up from scratch.

If all entrepreneurs matriculated via the route of the enterprising individuals—the Bostic method—we would be a nation of very efficient little PepsiCos. We would no longer have a need for such American institutions as Chapter 11 and bank work-out departments. Ma and Pa would refer to family members only, and not to a traditional business partnership. The Steven Jobses of this world would first get their M.B.A.'s, followed by a stint with Big Blue. The family garage as a laboratory would be but a piece of faded American history.

And, oh yes, small business would be significantly more efficient and professional than it is today.

But what would happen to those of us who have a gnawing need—The Urge—to own our own businesses, but who can't, or won't, get an M.B.A. or punch PepsiCo's clock? Without the requisite arsenal of education and experience, would we be doomed to fall through capitalism's cracks, pumping gas or bagging groceries after jettisoning our dreams in midair?

Sorry, Bostic, but we dice rollers do have a place reserved for us in the capitalistic system. Our role is—through creativity, unrestricted free thinking, and often logic-defying risk taking—to start up those embryonic companies that ultimately grow to become the candidates for your professional management. Mix our unsophisticated creativity with the lack of preconceived notions, add a dash of pioneering spirit, and you have the ruddy-cheeked, willing-to-risk-it-all, gunslinging entrepreneur.

The economic downside that results from our lack of sophistication is a high mortality rate and a distinct waste of motion in the process. But the upside is that we eventually bring to the marketplace the kind of companies that enterprising individuals and professional managers love to buy, but could never, or would never, give birth to themselves.

Occasionally, the entrepreneur is capable of making the transition to professional manager. More often, however, as in my case, we are not, and our company's leadership is then passed to the enterprising individuals waiting hungrily for us to say "uncle."

Thus we have an orderly process of business evolution—a proven and sensible process. Entrepreneurs need enterprising individuals standing in the wings, and enterprising individuals need entrepreneurs to sort out the wheat from the chaff and create opportunities. Both have their unique strengths. Often, the very strengths that ensure entrepreneurial success hinder the attempt to become a professional manager. Ditto for the professional manager attempting to create a start-up.

The truth of the matter is that everybody brings something to the table in today's survival-of-the-fittest economy. Entrepreneurs have their role, and professional-managers-turned-enterprising-individuals have theirs. We both survive because we both are necessary to the evolution of American business.

You can bet your balance sheet there will always be a ready supply of entrepreneurs as long as we have a capitalistic system. Many of us will continue to spend too much of our time jousting with windmills and trudging uphill against the wind, as we do today. Many will continue to be satisfied with the less lofty goals of feeding the family and paying the bills—creating as we go something from nothing, while providing opportunities for caring employees.

You heard it here: The species *entrepreneur* will prevail.

Meanwhile, let's hope that American resourcefulness discovers a way to better educate us gunslinging entrepreneurs, allowing more of us to make the professional manager transition and thus compete on a level playing field with the enterprising individuals. Most of us would welcome any assistance.

We do, however, reserve the right to fall madly in love with our companies, employees, customers, and niches. We also reserve the right to persevere for the sake of creativity and growth, and nothing more.

If we should happen to build equity and value along the way, so much the better.

# Index

Accidental entrepreneur, 242
Accountability, 17, 22, 113–15
  and inventory, 153
Accountants, 53, 70–74
  and board of directors, 76
Account executives, 12, 63–64
Accounting department, 119
  personnel, 51
Accounting firms, 33
Accounting systems, 21
  problems, 110
  and salespeople, 91
Accounts payable clerks, 12
Adidas, 97
Administrative issues, 13
Advertising, 33
Advisory board, 77
Ainsworth-Land, George T., 7, 8, 9
American Compensation Association,
  118
Angels, 39–40
Appreciation, 116
Arbitration, 200
Art department, 129
Asset management
  and compensation, 118
  problems, 110
Assets, 50, 65, 148
  sale of, vs. stock sale, 200
  and selling price, 191, 203
Attendance, 119

Audit, and selling business, 196
Availability, 133, 154

Balance, 22, 106–8
Balance sheet, 15, 16, 17, 65, 148
  and bankers, 66
  and business plan, 33
  and Phase III, 20, 24, 25
  and start-up financing, 37, 38
Bankers, 12, 16, 51, 73, 196
  and board of directors, 76
  and business plan, 33
  finding and keeping, 62–66
  and inventory, 153
  and Phase III, 19–20
  and start-up financing, 37–38
Barriers to entry, 33
Big Six (national) accountants, 71–
  72, 73
Blanchard, 133, 159
Board of directors, 75–77
Bonuses, 118, 120
Bookkeeping, 50
  and inventory, 153
Books, and training, 123–24
Borrowing base, 16
Bostic, Steve, 241–42, 243
Bottlenecks, 19
Breach-of-contract covenants, 200,
  203
Budgets, 50, 156–57, 158

Burnout, 24
Business, small
 acquisition of, and corporate culture, 108
 avoiding most painful mistakes, 139–74
 case history of, 11–27
 keys to success in, 85–135
 selling, 24–27, 187–207
 start-up, 31–44
 three phases of evolution, 7–10
Business appraiser, 188
Business associates, 76
Business broker, 188, 190, 192, 194
Business deals, records and, 43–44
Business plan, 31–35, 42
 and financing, 38, 40

Capital
 availability of, 134, 211
 cost of, 134
 sources, 33
 start-up, 38–41
Career decisions, 177–83
Cash, 26–27
 unwritten rule of, 202–4
Cash flow, 15
 in business plan, 33
 and inventory, 17
 managing, 148–50
 and Phase III, 19
 projections, 17, 24
Cash manager, 50
CEOs, 181
CFOs, 15, 50, 110, 215, 235
 and expense control, 156, 158
 hiring, 52–53, 72, 140
 and inventory, 152
Change
 coping with, 86, 132–35, 236

 in corporate culture, 108–9
 strategic, 236
Chapter 7, 224–25, 226
Check signing, 44
Clarity, 22, 110–12
Commission
 and compensation issues, 117–18
 and profitability, 92
 schedules, 17
Commitment to sell, 187–88
Communication, 126–31
 of expectations, 114, 115
 skills, 53, 211
Compatibility, 86
Compensation, 116–21
 and balance, 107
 and business plan, 33
 and expense control, 157
Competition, 8, 32, 33, 48, 156, 196, 211, 215
Computers, 21, 51
Conflict
 and accountability, 114, 115
 avoidance, 167–69
 and quality, 97
Consultants, 22, 123
 and board of directors, 76
 finding and using, 78–80
Controllers, 50
 hiring, 72
Controls, 20, 21
 repairing, 22
Corporate culture
 changing, 17, 22
 and communication, 129
 control over, 222–23
 and customer reverence, 88–93
 developing balanced, 106–9
 and expense control, 156, 158
 and inventory, 152
 inventorying, 108–9
 and quality, 95

roots in UPS Years, 13–14
after sale of business, 206
and synergy, 130
Corporate entrepreneur, 242–43
Corporate résumé, 188–89
Costs, and quality, 96
CPAs, 53. *See also* Accountants
Cray, Seymour, 3
Creation, 230, 231
Creativity, 243
Credit
 policies, 21, 110
 sources, 33
Crisis management, 170–72, 177
Cross training, 124
Customers, 33, 222–23, 230
 and board of directors, 76, 77
 changing relationships with, 133
 feedback system, 91
 key, 90
 and Phase I, 11, 12, 14
 and Phase II, 16
 and Phase III, 19
 and product, 48
 and quality, 97
 records, 44
 revering, 3, 88–93, 236
 and sale of business, 196
 and start-up financing, 37
Customer service department, 89, 90,
 92–93
Cycles, 17

Damage-control measures, 21–23
Danger signals, 17
Debt, 211, 213–14, 217
Debtors, 44
Delegation
 and Phase II, 16, 18
 and start-up details, 43, 44
 and superstars, 85
Demographics, 32

Dependables, 116, 117
Design decisions, 89
Details
 and expenses, 158
 and hiring process, 139
 hiring someone to handle, 54–55
 and quality, 97
 and start-up, 42–44
Distribution, 33, 42, 48
Dividends, 32
Due diligence, 192–93, 195–98, 204

Earnings reports, 101
Economy, 211
Educational entrepreneur, 242
80/20 rule, 157
Employees, 14, 25, 230
 accountability, 114–15
 adapting to sales growth, 17, 21
 and business plan, 33
 and clarity of mission, 111–12
 and communications, 127–30
 and compensation, 116–21
 firing, 144–47
 hiring, 139–43
 inventorying and replacing, 22
 -involvement programs, 119
 key, 16, 17, 22, 89, 130, 140–41,
  165, 196, 197
 meetings, 129
 morale, 21
 ownership, 99–102, 134
 performance reviews, 130
 and quality, 98
 records, 43
 rights, 134
 and sale of business, 191, 192, 197,
  205–6
 and start-up financing, 37
 and strategy implementation, 164–
  65, 166
 and stress of rapid growth, 17

Employees (*cont'd*)
  training, 124
  upgrading, 17, 18
  *See also* Superstars
Entrepreneurs
  changes in, 132–33
  defined, 4–6, 218–20
  defense of, vs. managers, 241–44
  endurance of, 211–17, 229–31
  function during Phase II, 18
  likes and dislikes, 219–20
  vs. managers, 117–79
  replacing, 22, 174, 179
  style of, 211–28
  terror, 227–28
  and training, 122–24
  upgrading, 22–23
  ultimate downside, 224–26, 243
  ultimate upside, 221–23, 243
Equipment, 42, 65, 162
Equity, 16, 25, 148
ESOPs, 101, 120, 134
Ethics, 14, 135, 198, 236
Executives, 116, 118
Expenses, 50, 155–58

Fees
  accountants', 71–72, 73
  business brokers', 190
  consultants', 79
  lawyers', 69, 204
Financial person, and start-up, 50–53
Financial projections
  and banker, 65
  in business plan, 33
Financial statements, 20, 25, 51, 72–73
  communicating, to employees, 128
Financial understanding, 211
Financing
  and board of directors, 77
  start-up, 36–41, 42

Firing, 18, 144–47
  consultants, 79
First National Bank of Minneapolis, 63
Five-year plan, 34
Fixed assets, 33
Focus, 22, 158, 172, 237
  business plan and, 33
  defined, 160
  and hiring, 139
  problems with, 159–61
  and quality, 97
Follow-up, 114, 115, 124, 125, 152, 158
Forecasts, 50
Friends and relatives
  and board of directors, 76
  and start-up financing, 38–39

Game-breaking positions, 235
Gates, Bill, 103
Global economy, 133, 155
Goals, 128
  and business plan, 33
  defining, 111
  and performance, 17
  upgrading, 22
Government regulations, 13, 134
*Grow or Die* (Ainsworth-Land), 7
Growth, 230, 231
  adapting to, 21, 162–63
  and hiring superstars, 86
  phases, 7–23
  rapid, 79–80, 162
Guarantees, 213–14
  to banker, 65, 66

High-tech, narrow niche, 103–4
Hiring, 18, 42
  financial person, 50–53
  process, 139–43
  sales staff, 90

skills, 211
someone to pick up pieces, 54–55
superstars, 86
for tomorrow, 22
Human resources, 51, 134

Industry information, 32
Information, 50, 116, 134
Inside players, 47–55
Insurance, 13, 43
Integration and diversification (Phase III), 20
Interviews, employee, 140–41, 142
Intuition, 211, 212–13, 217
Inventory, 17, 51, 65, 159
  and cash flow tracking, 149, 150
  control, 21
  just-in-time, 133, 153–54
  managing, 151–54
  problems, 110
  replacing sold, 37
  shrinkage, 152, 153
  valuation of, for sale of business, 192
Investors, 31–32, 33
Invoices, 159
IRS, 101

Job descriptions, 111–12
Job performance, 110–11
  annual review, 130
  and compensation, 118–19, 121
Job proposal, 142–43
Jobs, Steven, 3, 4, 103, 243
Job security, 116
Just-in-time inventory, 133, 153–54

Key employees, 16, 17, 89, 130
  and customer reverence, 89–90
  and hiring, 140–41
  inventorying and replacing, 22

and sale of business, 196, 197
and strategy meetings, 130, 165
Key players, 32, 38, 89–90

Landlord, 12
Lawyers, 25, 33, 65, 67–69, 73, 134, 218
  and board of directors, 76
  and firing employees, 146
  importance of using, 44
  and selling business, 189–90, 194, 199–200
  and stock deals, 100
Lease terms, 33, 43
Legal searches, 196
Letter of intent, 192
Liabilities, 148, 203
Licenses, 33, 44
LIFO write-downs, 110
Listening, 127, 131, 142
Litigation, 134
  and sale of business, 189, 192, 200, 206
Loan terms, 65
Local accountants, 71, 73
Location, 33
Low-tech, wide niches, 104, 151
Luck, 211

Management
  assembling team, 42
  contract, 193
  depth, 8, 20, 162
  going outside organization for, 22
  hiring, 72, 85–87
  information systems, 50
  and Phase II, 17
  quality, 8, 19, 20–21
  skills, 23, 236
  techniques, changes in, 133–34

Management (*cont'd*)
  training, 22, 124–25
Managers, professional
  and conflict, 168–69
  vs. entrepreneurs, 241–44
  and focus, 160–61
  hiring, 178–79
  transition from entrepreneur to, 19,
    26, 112, 177–79, 244
Manufacturing
  as marketing tool, 91
  and quality, 97
Marketing manager, 235
Marketing strategies, 33, 42, 91
Markets, defining, 164
Mentors, 59–61, 235
Minnesota Cooperation Office, 39
Minority shareholders, employees as,
  99–102
MIS, 152
Mission, 33, 128
  defining, 111
  upgrading, 22
Mistakes
  admitting, 236
  origins of most painful, 139–74
  in Phase I, 13
Motivation
  employee, 114–15, 116, 120–21
  entrepreneurial, 230–31
Movers and shakers, 116, 117–18
Murphy's Law, 20

National Business Incubations Asso-
  ciation, 40
National Screenprint, 39, 94, 95, 106,
  110, 162, 177
  evolution and growth of, 9
  Phase I of, 11–14
  Phase II of, 15–18
  Phase III of, 19–23

sale of, 24–27, 205–6
Networking, 72, 79
Newsletters, 129
Niche, 8, 11, 15, 17
  accountants', 73
  in business plan, 32, 38
  finding right, 103–5, 211

Office supplies, 51
Operations manager, 235
Optimism, 212, 214–16, 217
Organizational structure, 211
Organization charts, 17
Outplacement services, 146
Outside players, 59–80
Ownership, new, 193, 205–7

Pantsers, 14, 73
  vs. entrepreneurs, 5–6
Paper-flow systems, 21
  and inventory, 152
Patience, 172
Pay-for-performance plans, 118–19,
  121
Perks, 120
Personnel issues, 13, 17
Peter Principle, 16, 144, 173–74
Peters, Tom, 133, 159, 160, 163
Phase I (Entrepreneurial or UPS
  Years)
  case history of, 11–14
  defined, 8–9
Phase II (Norming or Sunshine
  Years), 14
  case history of, 15–18
  defined, 8–9
Phase III (Integrating or Years from
  Hell)
  case history of, 19–23, 24, 110
  defined, 8–10, 18, 20

Physical plant, 42
Planning, 111
  vs. crisis, 171, 172
  process, 163, 164–65
  and Phase III, 20
  *See also* Strategy
Policy manual, 128–29
President, hiring, 19, 25, 72, 160,
  179
Price/earnings multiples, 180, 182,
  190–91
Pricing, 33, 89, 91, 156
Private companies, 181–83
Procrastination, 44, 146
Product, 33
  champion, 47–79, 117–18
  and compensation, 118
  defining, 164
  development, 33, 42, 90
Production
  balance between sales and,
    106–8
  scheduling systems, 17
Productivity, 119
Profit-and-loss statements, 17, 24,
  148
  and bankers, 66
  in business plan, 33
  and quality program, 96
  and sales force, 91
Profits (profitability), 149
  and bonuses, 118, 119
  and business plan, 32
  communicating information to em-
    ployees, 128
  and Phase II, 16, 17, 18
Promotional plans, 33
Promotion from within, 22, 86
Public companies, 25, 180–83
Purchase agreement, 193, 199–201,
  203

Purchaser of business, researching,
  196–98
Purchasing manager, 235

Quality, 14, 17, 19, 236
  change in, 133
  commitment to, 94–98
  and compensation, 119
  control, 21
  selling, 91
Quarterly earnings report, 182

Real estate, 65
Receivables, 65
  financing, 37
  problems, 21, 110, 150, 151, 159
Receiving and inventory manage-
  ment, 153
Record-keeping, 43–44
References, employee, 52, 73, 139–
  40, 141
Regional accountants, 71
Relatives, 21, 38–39, 76
Résumé, corporate, 188–89
Return policies, 89
Returns on assets (ROA), 72–73,
  119–20
Returns on equity (ROE), 72
Returns on sales (ROS), 72
Revenue growth, 17
Revolvers, 116–17
Reward, in business plan, 32
Risk, 228
  and balanced culture, 108
  in business plan, 32
  downside, 226
  living with, 211, 213–14, 217
  and selling business, 189
Roster of players, 32, 38
Rules, bending, 90–91

Sales
  hiring team, 42
  importance of, 235–36
  meetings format, 91
  strategies, 33, 42
  techniques, changes in, 133
Sales department, 129
  balance between production and,
    106–8
  and communications, 127
  and compensation, 117–18
  and customer reverence, 89–90,
    92–93
  and financial person, 51, 52
  and inventory, 152, 153
  manager, 12, 235
Sales growth rate, 8
  adapting to, 162–63
  do not increase rule, 21
  and Phase II, 16, 17, 18
  and Phase III, 19, 20, 21
  rapidly increased, 79–80
Schooling, 123
Seed-capital funds, 40
Selling business, 24–27, 187–207
  after the sale, 205–7
  case history, 24–27
  setting selling price, 190–91, 203
Seminars, 22, 123, 124
Service, 14, 91
Service businesses, 151
Shareholders, 180–81, 182, 183
  deals, 44
  employees as, 99–102
  meetings, 101
Shipping
  and inventory, 153
  policies, 89, 97
Small Business Administration
  (SBA), 40, 150
Small Business Development Centers
  (SBDCs), 34

SBDC Connection, 34
Spouses, 81–82, 218
State and local government, 40
Stock
  options, 120
  selling, vs. assets, 200
  values, 101
Strategy
  in business plan, 33, 34
  and change, 22
  communicating, to employees,
    128–29
  defined, 163–64
  developing, 18, 111, 162–66
  and employee ownership, 100
  meetings, 165
Success
  keys to, 85–135
  skills required for, 211–17
  tips for, 235–37
Superstars
  building team of, 85–87
  and customer reverence, 89–90
  and hiring, 139–43
  positions requiring, 235
  and training, 122
Suppliers, 42
Synergy, 129–30
Systems
  failure of, 21, 162
  and Phase III, 19, 20
  repairing and replacing, 22
  upgrading, 17

Taxes
  corporate, 51
  and sale of business, 200
Teams, 16, 230
  building, 85–87
  and compensation, 118–19, 121
  training, 122
Technology, 155

-based start-ups, 40
and niche, 103–4
Tediousness, and quality, 97–98
Ten-year plan, 34
Timeliness, 52
Training
  employee, 17, 18, 22, 122–25
  for entrepreneur, 59
  and synergy, 130
Trends, 211
Tuition reimbursement, 124
Turnarounds, 236
Turner, Ted, 3

"Understanding Cash Flow" (SBA
  pamphlet), 150
Unions, 119
Urge, the, 212, 216–17, 243

Vacation pay, 13
Vendors, 25, 33, 42, 196, 237

and board of directors, 77
and business plan, 33
credit, 12, 33
and inventory management, 153–
  54
purchase orders, 157
records, 44
and training, 124
Venture capitalists, 32, 38

Wal-Mart, 156
Walton, Sam, 91
Weaknesses, and selling business,
  189, 190
Withheld payments, and selling busi-
  ness, 200–201
Working capital, 16
Workmen's comp, 13, 43, 151

Xerox, 123

Zero-base budgeting, 156–57, 158